I0558214

MARIANNE PADJAN

5X INTERNATIONAL AWARD-WINNING, BEST-SELLING AUTHOR

Real Estate Inside Out

Legal Disclaimer

Copyright © 2023 MPowered Voice Publishing. All rights reserved worldwide.

No part of this material may be used, reproduced, distributed or transmitted in any form and by any means whatsoever, including without limitation photocopying, recording or other electronic or mechanical methods or by any information storage and retrieval system, without the prior written permission from the author, except for brief excerpts in a review. This book is intended to provide general information only. Neither the author nor publisher provides any legal or other professional advice. If you need professional advice, you should seek advice from the appropriate licensed professional. This book does not provide complete information on the subject matter covered. This book is not intended to address specific requirements, either for an individual or an organization. This book is intended to be used only as a general guide, and not as a sole source of information on the subject matter. While the author has undertaken diligent efforts to ensure accuracy, there is no guarantee of accuracy or of no errors, omissions or typographical errors. Any slights of people or organizations are unintentional. The author and publisher shall have no liability or responsibility to any person or entity and hereby disclaim all liability, including without limitation, liability for consequential damages regarding any claim, loss or damage that may be incurred, or alleged to have been incurred, directly or indirectly, arising out of the information provided in this book.

Connect with MPowered Voice Publishing
www.MPoweredvoicepublishing.ca
www.magneticfm.com

Copyright © 2023 by MPOWERED VOICE PUBLISHING
All rights reserved. No part of this publication may be reproduced or transmitted in any form or by any means, electronic, or mechanical, including photocopying, recording, or by any information storage and retrieval system.

DEDICATION

I am dedicating this book to all of our clients current and in the future. They hold a vision which we hope to bring into reality.

REAL ESTATE INSIDE OUT

Acknowledgements

I would like to acknowledge all of the authors in this book for their valuable time and energy. Thank you so much for sharing your knowledge and your years of experience with us in this book. I am honoured to share this space with you and am excited to pass this incredible information on to our future clients, family, friends and children.

To all future students of real estate, we welcome your hunger and interest in calling on us for support and guidance.

I would like to take a moment to thank my coach Robert J Moore. Thank you for all your guidance and support in helping me create MPowered Voice Publishing.

My gratitude goes to the friends and clients who have trusted me in the past and will trust me in the future to allow me to help guide them through what would be their largest purchase and most valuable home.

Thank you also to all the readers for your interest and support of *Real Estate Inside Out* and for choosing us to help you with your next home or investment.

In Gratitude

Marianne

TABLE OF CONTENTS

FOREWORD

I am so happy about this book because you are going to learn core strategies to help you grow your knowledge about Real Estate, including lessons in mindset, marketing, mortgages, and even investing in dream vacation properties.

I've known Marianne Padjan for a number of years and consider her a valued friend and a talented coach. She positively impacts the lives she touches and loves to connect people helping them to enrich the quality of their life. Marianne has published many books within her MPowered Voice Publishing company that share real-life experiences and valuable lessons that include contributions from each and every one of her co-authors.

As an entrepreneur who has practised Holistic Leadership and Health Wealth lifestyle philosophies for over 35 years, I continue to be a life learner dedicated to spiritual self-development. When I think of personal development and quality of life, to me, it embraces body, mind and spirit along with core values of integrity, compassion, and having an open growth mindset. My philosophy opens doors for me in my thinking, and as a result, I have taken action and have been investing in real estate for over 30 years.

I experience the power of investing in real estate, and I've also seen the results in the lives of many colleagues, friends and clients who work toward achieving their life dreams, including Marianne. Individuals who dream of becoming an entrepreneur and creating financial freedom in their life who take action, get to grow in their journey and create their dream life for real. You get to create your life by design.

For me, that means contributing to others by providing beautiful homes for families, individuals and seniors to live in. It means aiding in the development of new housing for families and refugees in Canada and abroad and offering vacation retreats and villas that help people restore their health and healing. Investing in real estate is the one most successful entrepreneurial decision one can make; history teaches us this.

It takes many people from living month to month to better plan and secures their retirement funding, as well as their health and wellness needs, and it helps people become independent multi-millionaires.

I welcome you on this journey if you are thinking about investing in real estate, if you own one or more properties if you are a real estate or financial professional, or if you are seasoned in real estate because this book embraces lessons that will inspire you and offer you new and powerful perspectives.

Cheryl Lynn Ivaniski Dr.A., Ch.T, RDH

Accredited Real Estate Investor and Wealth Builder

Founder of Holistic Diabetes Solutions - Scholarship-based Training Program

Holistic Diabetes Coach - How to Naturally lower blood sugars and A1C's

Cheryl Ivaniski is recognized as a Health and Wealth Authority. Her Holistic Approach to life includes having a healthy mind, body and healthy finances. Cheryl is an accredited real estate investor who invests in residential and commercial properties, as well as businesses and franchises in North America and abroad.

She is a 7 X International best-selling author, a global award-winning author and a recipient of the prestigious Quilly Award. Cheryl is a Dr. Holistic Medicine, Dr. Traditional Chinese Medicine and Acupuncture, with advanced training in natural nutrition, mind-body hypnosis and NLP. In addition to her expertise in Wellness, Cheryl inspires, empowers and educates women and men with safe, proven, natural solutions that teach people how to lower and balance their blood sugar levels naturally for life. She is the creator of her 4-Step proprietary process, the *"Diabetes Success System"* (Signature coaching program), that is transforming how people live with ease, peace of mind, confidence and predictable and consistent blood sugars so they can live their healthiest life. Cheryl is the founder of *Holistic Diabetes Solutions* and is a sought-after speaker and thought leader in the areas of Holistic Diabetes Wellness, self-empowerment and mindset transformation. In addition, Cheryl's 10-Step program for investing in real estate has mentored hundreds of students, helping them navigate the world of how to be a successful real estate investor.

To connect with Cheryl and learn more about her training programs, please visit

www.cherylivaniski.com
www.holisticdiabetessolutions.com

REAL ESTATE INSIDE OUT

VACATION PROPERTIES

Marianne Padjan

I was 50 years old when I got my real estate license. I am now 61; it's been a very exciting journey. A year ago, I decided I wanted to do international real estate, but I couldn't figure out how.

2020 was a great year and instigated a lot of shifting in the entire world. This grand shift opened up a lot of options. People were buying properties outside of the country more and more. All I know is that I wanted a piece of this action.

As always, I started thinking about it, and then all of a sudden, someone came to me and asked me if I was interested in properties in the Cayman Islands. I had a conversation with the rep there, and we created a situation where I would advertise and talk to people and send him the referrals, and I would collect a referral fee. I'm not licensed to work in another country but I can refer the person to someone who is and so that's what I did.

Later on that same month, I got approached by someone in the Dominican Republic for the same system. Then I got approached by someone from Costa Rica, then Mexico, then Belize.

It's funny when you make a decision, then all these opportunities start coming. As in life, you make yourself magnetic to these things, and they just come to you without any effort.

For me, it's important that I work with integrity, and so, of course, I would not represent all of these countries as different politics apply in each one, and some are more complicated than others.

If I'm going to refer a client or a friend, I want to make sure the company is reputable and has been around for a while. As it turns out, we are having a home show In Toronto, and one of the clients will have a booth there. I'm going to visit them to actually meet some of them in person. It's very exciting working internationally because these are properties that are an extra luxury for people so it's a lot easier to work with.

Many of these companies offer financing directly through them, so that makes everything a lot easier. Others have Canadian banks within their country to make things smoother. Also, many of my clients will purchase more than one property, so usually financing isn't an issue for these people. This, of course, makes my life a lot easier.

The way people buy their vacation homes, whether they're in the same country or outside the country, is pretty much the same as the way that they have bought their current homes that they are living in. The homes change, but the personalities of the people buying them remain the same.

If you have a habit of looking at details, decide on the most important features you want in a vacation home. If you only look at the big picture and you just want a home on the beach, you'll be a little more easily satisfied and a little less picky. This will probably not change.

You will probably typically act the same when you're looking for a vacation property. Some people have one criterion — I'd like it right on the beach, please. Others are more interested in such things as —is there a shuttle? Is there a bus? Is there a market? Are there stores? Are there bars or restaurants close by? Some will require that North American-style foods be close by, while others will prefer that only local-type foods are available.

People are people no matter where they are. Each person is different and has different requirements. The only similarity is that this, of course, is typically a second, third or fourth home for someone, so they look at it a little bit differently.

Their financing is typically a little stronger than, let's say, one of a first-time home buyer. It is typically more fun looking for a vacation property than it is for a first-time home. Certainly, there are requirements, but it's more about what people would like as opposed to what they need.

With investors, however, it's always a slightly different story as they typically purchase one, two, or more properties. Other than a few basic necessities, they don't care too much about what it looks like or what it is. There's no emotional attachment there. It's strictly about the dollars as they will only be renting it out or Airbnb it. It's there to make money. It's there for them to leave in their will to their family, children or grandchildren.

With others, it's a goal for retirement, and so they spend most of their life accumulating properties and then they have created a very nice retirement nest egg for themselves.

Since 2020, numerous people have been moving outside of the city and, in many cases, outside of the country as they are able to work from home. This has now been placing vacation homes in a much stronger position than where they were many years ago.

For many instead of having two or even three properties, many people have now opted to have just one, and that one in the place where they would typically vacation. The energy of people has changed and the way that they look at life.

The younger generation is looking to move farther and farther away from the city, getting closer and closer to living in places where they can have gardens they can create to grow their own food. They want their children to grow up in a friendly community where everyone is super neighbourly and looks out for each other, as in the city, things are typically much different.

As an agent, I find myself working much more outside of the city than inside of the city than I once did. And even if people are still living in the city, their investments seem to be going more and more outside of the city.

Whether or not they're planning on retiring there later, they seem to prefer having something a little further outside of the city as it's much more affordable. There are also many more builders building outside the city, so therefore, the properties are going up in price in many cases a lot faster.

Life in the last few years has changed for many people, and therefore the face of real estate has also changed. More and more people are going outside of the city, and more and more builders are building outside of the city; therefore, many more agents are selling outside of the city.

Life has changed in many ways, and it's my job to go with the flow and move into an area that is now up and coming more and more each day. Also, many of my existing clients feel more comfortable with me selling them properties rather than going off to a new agent that they don't know.

Real Estate, like all else in life, changes with the requirements of our clients, and we need to stay flexible and move with the market status. Life changes, as do we, and therefore so does the world around us. It's more interesting this way and more fun; it's always good to challenge ourselves.

Marianne Padjan

MARIANNE has been helping people with their real estate needs for 10-plus years. She has been a partner with EXP REALTY BROKERAGE for almost two years now. She enjoys helping people find their homes and investment properties.

Marianne also enjoys writing as she is a 5-time International Best-Selling Award-Winning author, CEO of MPowered Voice Publishing, co-Owner at MagneticFM radio, with *REAL ESTATE INS and OUTS* BOOK, RADIO SHOW and TV Podcast show.

Marianne has impacted many lives, both professionally as well as personally. She has guided clients from divorce to marriage as well as from bankruptcy to millionaire. She enjoys engaging people in their own growth so that they may discover their power and thrive! She also hosts a women's group MPowered Resilient Women International, where a high-end group of women inspire each other to do even better. Marianne is now also an executive contributor as well as on the expert panel and PR at Brainz Magazine.

As an empowerment coach, she also enjoys facilitating workshops and retreats as well as masterminds.

marianne.padjan@exprealty.com

mariannepadjan.exprealty.com

https://mariannepadjan.exprealty.com/

MASTERING FLIPPING

Victor Vetro

I come from a family of three children, and my parents always worked harder than I knew that I wanted to. We had everything we needed, but I decided that I wanted more. I like knowing that I can buy pretty much anything I want or need. To me, this meant I never had to stress or worry about money.

For the past thirty-plus years, I have been an entrepreneur working as a contractor. While I have done quite well, the rocky road to getting to this point was quite exciting. The journey was filled with good, great, and bad times! Sometimes you do great as the property is easy to renovate, all the papers and legalities are in place, and the real estate market is doing well. Other times you hit a road bump or bumps. Landing an estate sale is always fun as it consumes far too much time, and you never know what you will get. Or, other times, you make a purchase, and a recession starts before your closing date.

2020 brought about an exceptional shift for much more than the construction industry. Materials started being less and less available. This was not only irregular but very difficult to work with as it made it almost impossible to estimate how much a project would cost me when passing along a quote to a client. Guesstimating is not my style at all; my integrity is too important to me.

I have made some mistakes that have cost me both time and money in the past, and now I help others with my experience and mastery of the business. As in every industry, we learn as we go along. I consider myself to be a well-educated expert in flipping homes as a result of my amazing accomplishments. Overall, it has been a great career. I chose well for myself! I did well at doing something that I really enjoy. This industry gives me an opportunity to be super creative while making a good living, and I get to have new locations all the time.

There is a special kind of excitement when taking a messed-up house and turning it into a beautiful creation. I pride myself in doing impeccable work, and everyone always - yes, I said ALWAYS, admires my work, and all my projects sell quickly and for high prices. Kitchens are my specialty, as I enjoy showcasing them the most. It takes a special attention to detail to create a great kitchen, which is why I make and design my own, and as a result, they are spectacular!

I enjoy seeing my clients or buyers happy. I have had the pleasure of meeting some wonderful people on my path, not only the clients but also my Real Estate agents, lawyers and mortgage agents, and, of course, my team that works with me on the actual sites.

Renovations are fun, and you should try it if you are wanting to enter the flipping market.

Victor Vetro

Victor Vetro is a contractor who enjoys his craft so much that he says that he will never retire. He is truly a master at flipping as he has a talent second to none.

If you are interested in a Kitchen by Victor, then please connect with Marianne Padjan.

THE PATHWAY TO CREATE MILLIONS ... LIKE ME

Jennifer Jones

"For one to fly, one needs only to take the reins."

Most people have the recipe for success backward.

They wait to see success before they believe in it. I am here to tell you that it's the other way around. You must first believe in your success before you can ever truly see it.

That's what I call magic, and it can be utilized by anyone who wishes for greatness – especially those who want to play the game of life at the highest level.

To introduce myself, my name is Jennifer Jones. I became a licensed realtor in 2014. I started renovating and flipping properties in my twenties in both Florida and Ontario, Canada, prior to getting licensed, and that's when I saw the power of real estate. I was buying homes, condos, and cottages that needed a little love and fixing them up, giving them a complete makeover and selling them at a much higher price.

Everything I had been taught about having the money prior to spending money had been a lie! The truth was, to make money, I needed to borrow money. After buying and selling real estate with Realtors, I realized I just needed to get licensed. By the time I had reached my third year as a Realtor, I ended up making over $1,125,000 in Gross Commission Income as an individual agent. This is no easy feat, as many in real estate will tell you, and it does not happen often. I'm here to tell you anyone can do it.

My success quickly helped me get recognized as the top agent in our Brokerage and Province and the 2nd best agent in all of

Canada. By my fourth year, I had agents approaching me to join the team and help handle all the clients. Over the next four years, our team grew to over forty realtors with fifteen incredible office support rockstars! What made us different was our approach -- we focused on agents who were hungry to serve others and on a personal growth journey. These are agents who are also either invested in real estate or looking to get started. That way, we could provide the team with more tactics, strategies, and blueprints to creating wealth rather than just selling more homes (which

is what most teams and brokerages do).

I do not want to state my track record to brag. It is to simply impress upon you that it was built from the ground up in a very short amount of time. If I can do it, then you can too!

In the pages ahead, I will take you on a journey. I want to invite you into my world and show you the pathway to millions. Your ability to obtain wealth will be heavily based on your level of faith. Remember, you must first believe before you can succeed. Are you ready? If so, let's saddle up for one heck of a ride. After all, your magic is waiting.

We need to have an abundance mentality; that is what we teach our agents. If we think from a place of scarcity, we are operating with fear and apprehension, but if you work on faith and with love, you will find abundance, and that is what is magical about this job, and really, it guides you in life as well. It will show in your dealings and communications with the clients as well. Clients can tell when you have faith in the relationship and when you have established trust; it speaks volumes more than signing a piece of paper ever could. I feel like agents who work relentlessly try to lock in their clients are doing themselves a disservice; it is a desperate move, and it appears so to the client as well.

The truth is, when you CARE, you set yourself apart from everyone else. You offer your clients trust, which is rare

in this world, and compassion. You show them that you value them for who they are rather than what they can give you. You shine apart from the others when you show them you care, by giving options, by giving them advice and having their best interests at heart. You show it by doing little things like getting coffee and big things like giving ten thousand dollars out of pocket to a client who couldn't sell their house because the buyers kept insisting on reducing the price by 10k. This helped them buy their dream home. When you do good things, good things come back to you; it is what I have always believed in. They might not come back from the same person, but they come back nonetheless.

You set yourself apart with this exemplary customer service, and that is memorable. When you're memorable for the right reasons, people come back, they recommend you to their friends and families, and that is what keeps your business going. You just have to CARE.

When you have an abundance mindset, you understand how important and how joyous giving to others truly is. When you open your heart and give freely to others, without expecting anything in return, the rewards you reap from that are magnified tenfold. Whether the universe rewards you, or God, I firmly have faith that the kindness that you put out into the world comes back to you, no doubt about it.

We have always aspired to provide our clients with the highest level of service, and that means going above and beyond to make sure our customers are happy and feel cared for. Whenever we go over to a client's house, we always call beforehand and ask them if they need something. I'd ask them if I could pick them up a coffee or tea or anything from the store. We always gift a client a five-dollar lottery gift card whenever we meet them and say 'I hope you get lucky.' These small gestures don't take a lot for us to do, but they mean a lot to the client. You laugh and joke with them and talk to them and share your plans, but do all of this without having any expectations, without the expectation of signing even one contract.

You want to show the clients that you want to do right by them, to show them that you just want the best for them, human to human. We do a lot for our communities as well, without expecting anything in return. We host free coffee events, and all it says on the card is 'pay it forward.' So, we will randomly put a lot of money into different coffee shops, and if you go there that day and put in your breakfast order, you won't be asked to pay, but instead, you'll be handed this card with the message 'pay it forward.' We might include a little joke in it so that it becomes evident that we don't expect any payment in return, except in the form of kindness to others.

We do this in hopes of inspiring some positivity and happiness in the community so that the people might go about their day in a slightly better mood than they were in when the day started. We might get some business as a result of doing this, but that is not our main intention. We just do it because we want to make people happy. We donated fourteen thousand dollars to the food bank; we don't want anything in return, and we don't get anything back from these places, obviously, except the joy and satisfaction of giving to others. I donate quite frequently to different charities that help animals around the world. I love all animals, great or small, and that is a cause that is near and dear to my heart.

We sponsor a lot of teams from local communities. We don't get any direct business from these activities a lot of the time, but we do it because we believe in pouring energy into the community and taking care of the people that live in the community we work in, and when we do, it always comes back to us 100-fold. I completely believe that one of the reasons why we are so successful is because we operate from a place of genuine love and compassion. We aren't just a cold corporation that is only concerned about its bottom line at the end of the day, we are in the business of serving people, and we can only do a good job of that when we deal with them with love and care.

Deals come and go. You can't get too attached to that. I actually got one of my first businesses from helping someone else out. I was getting to know these elderly people who needed their garage doors painted. I just saw it as an opportunity to help these people, to do something kind for them, and I realized that when you build your business around kindness and helping people, you get a unique insight into how you can actually be of service to them. I kept wondering how I could connect with the people around me, what their businesses were and, what I could do to get them more business, how I could promote them. I still do that; now, we have the luxury of not expecting anything in return.

You can help others out in any capacity, no matter what your job is. We have a plumber that we work with who's a really great guy who will go to any lengths to help the clients. He told me that if I knew anyone who really couldn't afford to pay their bills, or if somebody is elderly or sick, I could just let him know, and he would take care of them right away.

That kind of energy is so genuine and so amazing, and I love that because that is exactly the kind of energy that I hope to inspire and have. I really feel grateful that I have attracted an amazing group of people that I work with, that we all believe in helping out, and we all operate from the same place where we love to give to others without expecting any kind of recognition or reward in return.

You might think that because I have been blessed with this life of abundance, doing something like this is easier for someone like me. You might say, well, it's fine when you do it, but I can't because I can barely pay my bills. It has nothing to do with what you can afford and everything to do with what you can contribute. If you're a janitor, you could offer to help a sick or elderly person clean up their house for free. If you're a teacher, you can help tutor a struggling family's kids for free. If you're a musician, you can play for sick children in the hospital. There is always something you can do.

You can't put the cart before the horse; you have to change your mindset because people can sense who the genuine givers are and who is operating from scarcity; they can tell the real deal from the pretentious and unwilling.

You want to be known as someone who is a giver. It gives you a sense of identity, a personal brand, so to speak. People want you in their life in some capacity because they know you won't end up using them.

You don't need money to be a giver. You can donate your knowledge, your time, or a sympathetic ear. You could just go and spend time with someone who is sick, struggling or lonely. If you're a giver, you will find opportunities to show people that you're there for them, to show that you have love them and you want to help take care of them. It could be something as simple as picking up coffee for them or offering to mow their lawns.

There are so many community groups you can reach out to to donate your time. You can volunteer at an animal shelter. The furry babies love spending time with humans; they are so starved for love and affection; all you have to do is go spend an hour with them, and you will make their day.

You can volunteer at the soup kitchen or deliver meals to people who are sick, or volunteer at the hospice. The options are many, and you can do something that you feel you would genuinely enjoy doing.

Even though you're not doing any of this for your business or expecting to get anything in return, people see your involvement and, in turn, want to support your business.

They see that you care for them and the community, so they, in turn, support your business to show their appreciation. It is not the goal of doing this, but it is the universe's way of rewarding you for your good deeds. You will also meet other people who have a similar energy to you, who love helping out and who are givers, and meeting such people will boost your own energy levels and improve your vibrations.

It might sound very spiritual, but that is what it is. It is a universal spiritual law. You will attract givers if you start giving, and you will learn to recognize and repel takers. Takers are energy vampires; they want to deplete you of your energy and take as much as they can from you. They want to take your time, your energy, and use you in any way that they can because they don't care because they only think about themselves. So, by being a giver, you emanate this positive energy that attracts other positive people toward you.

Even though we don't give for the sake of getting rewards, the universe will reward you for your good deeds and positive spirit. You might not get anything back from the people you help, nor should you, because these people need help, they don't have to give you anything, but the universe will pay you back in other ways to show its appreciation. So in order to create mind-blowing success, the answer is "First Believe" and live your life as if you are already living in abundance and work to "give before you receive," having no attachment to anything.

Jennifer Jones

Jennifer Jones is the principal of *"The Jennifer Jones Team,"* which has been climbing to the top of The Toronto Real Estate Board (currently sitting in the Top Ten Spots out of 70,000 Realtors) and the Top of EXP Realty Teams.

Jennifer's strength has been in attracting talented management who have helped create the strategies, systems, accountability, personal growth, mindset improvement, and training systems to create a model that can be duplicated to help any agent create individual success or structure their own team into success.

Jennifer and her husband, Keith, own multiple rental properties and invest in Storage Units and Commercial properties throughout North America. Jennifer is a Public Speaker, Coach, and Best-Selling Author on Amazon. She and her husband currently reside in King City, Ontario, with their standard poodle Mike. They enjoy time with their two grown children and recent grandchildren.

WHY DIY MARKETING SHOULDN'T BE DONE ALONE

Tammy Williams

Ask yourself these questions:

Would I perform heart surgery on myself?

Would I perform my own root canal?

Would I build a house by myself?

If you answered no to any of the questions, then you are part way there. As an individual that has worked in sales marketing roles for 15 + years, it was very apparent to me, along with my managers, colleagues and staff, that our roles were essential to the company's growth and survival. Since we know success leaves clues, it is very surprising to see many entrepreneurs that have taken DYI too far.

Contrary to what some believe, marketing is not easy, and it can't be done by everyone.

I recall a recent consultation call that I had with a prospect that had several events and products that want help marketing to create brand awareness and plant seeds. Before any marketing begins, the foundation has to be in place, just like building a solid house. We went through a series of questions, things like goals, mission, what solutions they solve and then on to the website etc. They already had a website - a standard 5-page website that they had paid good money for.

Sadly after assessing the website, I discovered there wasn't enough content, nor was there enough of the keywords for their product/industry to come up in an online search, no C.T.A.s (Call To

Action), no live video, no testimonials and 80% of the website was about the owner YAWNNNNNNNNNNNNNN.

Although they agreed and liked many of my suggestions, in the end, they decided the dollar amount to make the necessary improvements was too much for them. They chose to have flyers created to use to market their events and products.

Our conversation surrounding their goals and what they placed value in, along with how little value they saw in investing in marketing, shed light on their mindset because everything was viewed as a cost rather than an investment in their business. Although I could have sold them on why they should implement my suggestions, I chose not to. The truth of the matter is it's the client's decision, right or wrong. The entrepreneur/business owner should have an investor mindset with short-term and long-term goals, along with realizing that most successful people in business have people that work with them with different expertise.

To not invest money in marketing and website improvements is like leaving the house door open while you go on vacation and expecting it to be okay without giving it any attention. No one would start their business without wise counsel, without knowing what they need as far as finances, location etc., so why not get access to the intellectual property of a marketing professional?

It makes me think of individuals that buy million-dollar-plus homes, and choose the bargain basement in pricing in-home security systems. Buying a home is the largest purchase a person can make, so why a bargain basement-priced home security system?

Time and time again, myself and some of my colleagues see many start-ups and existing businesses without a sales/marketing budget, or the dollar amount allotted is less than what is required. It's important for the potential client to see the value in having a marketing specialist or a marketing team. It could save you time and make your marketing efforts more impactful.

Some of the benefits of marketing:

- generate leads

- increase your brand awareness

- make your business memorable

- let your potential clients know what your company is all about

- promote your services/products

- assist with the sales process

- make you stand out amongst your competitors

- make clients buy rather than make them feel like they are being sold to.

Entrepreneurs need to see marketing as an investment in their business instead of seeing it as a "cost."

A conversation surrounding goals leads to the mindset of the potential client. It goes without saying that goals are important. The mindset of the entrepreneur is key. It may sound odd to hear the word mindset. You may be wondering why the mindset would be important. Depending on how seasoned an individual is, I give them a questionnaire that I developed, "YOUR CTA." It's a series of questions to help me and the potential client understand where they are in valuing or devaluing marketing. The questions are based on how they value their time, and goals, how they feel about delegating, and what dollar value they put on securing a client. This is a great learning tool for both parties to see if they are on the same page.

It's important to know the following:

Talent.com reports that salaries in the United States for all marketing jobs combined range from $35,115 per year to $100,000 per year.

A person working in Marketing in Canada typically earns around $134,000 CAD per year. Salaries range from $62,200 CAD (lowest average) to 222,000 CAD (highest average, the actual maximum salary is higher).

http://www.salaryexplorer.com/salary-survey.php?loc=38&loctype=1&job=36&jobtype=1

However, investing all of the money in the world without the right people to expedite the follow-up/follow-through is useless. Nothing happens without sales! Just like ebony and ivory on a keyboard, sales and marketing go hand and hand. They are very similar in that they are an important part of the customer's journey. Marketing helps to find and build rapport with prospects, while the sales strategy is to provide solutions and get the sale.

So what is marketing you ask?

Let's start with a few things that marketing isn't.

- Marketing isn't telemarketing
- Marketing isn't an afterthought
- Marketing isn't a listing in a business directory
- Marketing isn't selling before having a relationship

Simply put, marketing is a guide, a blueprint of sorts with various activities and actions to attract customers through engagement to walk them through an exemplary journey that converts them into paying customers.

Sales strategy is about positioning, following a sales process to put a potential client through the sales funnel, proper business, providing information, follow-ups, and follow-throughs.

A few things that marketing is:

- Marketing is engaging
- Marketing is building connections
- Marketing takes time and dedication
- Marketing is critical to business growth to stay fresh in the minds of potential clients

Here are a few of the hundreds of forms of marketing:

- Advertising,

  - Being interviewed

  - Direct mail

  - Email campaigns

  - Texting

  - What's App

  - Video Marketing

  - Influencer marketing

  - Speaking

  - Blog writing

  - Social media

  - Referral marketing

To my fellow entrepreneurs, here are some ways to make yourself stand out online:

- **Develop your brand identity.** The reason I suggest this is that many people change companies but stay in the same field, or sometimes there are company mergers. So developing your own brand is YOU, no matter what firm you work with. This includes a number of things, such as your company colours, name, and logo, allowing you stand out from your competition, with an image that stays cemented in the minds of potential customers. For example, think about Nike — their logo and tagline are recognizable all over the world. Even Walmart, along with their colours, is unforgettable, plus they have their famous slogan – "Rollback."

- **Have your very own personalized website** that is compatible to all devices - your customers are buying YOU. This is really important. It's like a resume but in website format and even more, because you can put more of your personality into it, keeping to the industry's standards. Please don't buy into the one-size fits all website package, think of your purpose for having one to start with along with asking yourself if you would want to know more after looking at it.

- **Optimize your website.** This can pretty much increase your customer's experience, conversion rate, ranking and more. Make sure it is compatible with mobile devices, keep it running smoothly, updated regularly, and speed up your site. Page speed is a main factor that increases google ranking. Over 40% of users expect a website to load in two seconds.

Check the speed of your website with:

GT Metrix

or

https://www.searchenginewatch.com/2019/01/03/google-pagespeed-insights-tool-100/

-You must have a consistent online presence to gain a larger reach

- Engage with people that like or comment on your posts

- Don't be all business; add some of your personal life, interests etc.

- Be memorable in a good way

- Keep it simple

- Create a content bank

- Use pleasing visuals and colours that go with your brand

The marketing that is considered old is still used today incorporating technology and social meeting. Since we know that marketing isn't a sale, it's important to remember that nothing happens without a sale. Many companies adopted the marketing mix to get the results they wanted. It has been documented that it has helped companies make strategic decisions.

The marketing mix that has been used for decades was developed in 1960 and is still a cornerstone today. The marketing mix refers to E. Jerome McCarthy's four Ps: Product, Price, Placement, and Promotion.

To conclude, don't hide behind social media or your ads-remember the purpose of a phone and a website.

Rather than thinking of the cost of marketing think about the cost involved if you don't do it.

Lastly, marketing is so important to the growth and survival of a business. Don't let it start and end with the marketing team. Many things can be a DIY, don't let your marketing be one of them.

Tammy Williams

Tammy Williams is a 4x International Best Selling Author with over 15 years in marketing and sales. She is a collaboration and sales/marketing leader that is great at providing solutions for clients, from existing businesses that are brick and mortar to those transitioning to click and order. She helps clients monetize their websites with various social media strategies and marketing campaigns. She is also a Business Mentor to graduating business students of *Access Employment* and is a proud member of *MP Resilient Women International Women Group*, Advisory Board Member for *Cameras For Girls*, a registered Charity.

She is the founder of *Women, Champagne and Real Estate* and *CryptoSmart Chicks*. The goal is to empower women with all things real estate and crypto. She believes we all can give and she started a Walk a Mile in her Shoes campaign several years ago and has been able to collect over 400 pairs of ladies' new and gently worn footwear which has been donated to various places in Durham region.

ABOLISH A NEGATIVE SELF-IMAGE

John Toublaris

"I AM. Two of the most powerful words. What you put after them shapes your reality." – Bevan Lee

Dealing with a Negative Self-Image

Beating myself up mentally, and making myself feel flawed, was a constant habitual pattern in my life from my childhood background. The constant negative self-talk of *"I am not good enough; I am not smart enough; I don't think I can succeed as well as they can; I don't have what it takes to be successful;"* and on and on was an automatic way of thinking about myself.

The mental picture I formed in my mind was that everyone else was better than me, and I wouldn't amount to much in my life. The feelings of inadequacy became stronger and stronger, and consequently, I would take fewer positive actions in my life. I remember people telling me, "Stop thinking so big; if you think so big, you will lose out on the smaller things in life." Others were constantly telling me to "Just go get a regular job." Later in my real estate career, even though I wanted to be so successful, I would be hesitant, and I would judge others because I was judging myself. I would tell myself, "That seller won't be choosing you tonight, so why bother going on the listing presentation?" I avoided calling on For Sale by Owners because of my self-talk, "There are so many other Realtors in the city; why would they ever choose me?" When calling my database, I would tell myself, "I will sound like a fraud if I call them." I didn't want that; therefore, I would do something else, and the avoidance behaviour would kick in.

Furthermore, anytime I would take any action, and if it did not go as well or as planned, I would blame myself and beat myself up. My self-esteem would diminish and take me completely out of whatever I was up to, and I never went back to it.

These thoughts formed from an early age from my parents constantly wanting to do things for me. Then, when they would show me how to do something, and I didn't do it 100% as they wanted it done, they would dwell on any mistake and make it my fault. I developed a belief that I was incapable of doing anything on my own. Later in life, these deep-rooted beliefs would cost me dearly, in both my personal life and my career. I was in suspended animation, held hostage to my emotional immaturity. However, today, I have realized that my parents love me, and wanted, and still do want, the best for me. They did their best with what they knew at that time.

The Turnaround

I made a decision to find out why I was a prisoner to these self-deprecating, disparaging thoughts. I had no specific plan, only that I did not want to live life in the shadows. I stumbled into many programs, focused briefly on many new business concepts, and eagerly engaged in several self-discovery seminar/workshop programs. I took the time and necessary actions, from simple naiveté, to increase my self-awareness. I began to shift my thoughts quickly.

The truth is, these thoughts still come into my mind; however, two things are different for me now. First, I catch them quicker than I did before. When I do catch them, I laugh about it because I identified it rather than having that thought control and take over the moment. The instant it happens, I shift my focus by asking myself quality questions. For example, if that thought comes in as, "I won't be successful at that," I will bring doubt in to weaken the belief in such a way as, "How do I know if that is 100% true? How do I really know?" When that belief weakens, I then ask myself, "If I were to be successful at that, how would that make a difference in my life today?" So, I now shift my focus to an empowering state. You can do the same.

Being kind and gentle towards myself took a long time. I first began with just a simple step. Day by day, as I began to think more positively about myself, I took notice and began to make small shifts in my life. I was committed to living with healthy and supportive thoughts. Remember, you are the person with whom you will have the closest relationship for your whole life. Make that commitment today, and be kind and gentle with yourself; because, when you do, you will attract the many wonderful gifts that life has to offer.

The Voice Inside Your Head

That nasty, brutal, crushing voice inside your head wants to morph with you and make you think it is really a part of your true essence. However, this voice is living like a parasite in your mind and is not part of your DNA. It did not come down the birth canal with you. Sadly, over time, you were groomed with insecurity and doubt, gathered from the negative circumstances of your life. Like most of us, you are aware of your internal faultfinder. It is that voice in your head that judges you, doubts you, belittles you, and constantly tells you that you are not good enough. It says negative, hurtful things to you—things that you would never even dream of saying to anyone else, "I am such an idiot; I am a phony; I never do anything right; I will never succeed."

Abolish a Negative Self-Image

The number one cause of low self-esteem and a negative self-image is the careless, insensitive comments by significant others in your life. Who is more significant to you than you? When someone else significant to you puts you down and verbally abuses you, it is emotional terrorism. However, when you nurse those thoughts and constantly ponder them, then you become your own worst enemy.

FREE BONUS

To crush that nasty voice inside your head so that you can feel good about yourself today, go to TheBookUnleashed.com, right now, under the Free Bonuses tab, to receive these powerful self-worth affirmations. These affirmations have helped my clients and me to abolish a negative self-image and feel confident and worthy.

The Difference Between Self-Image and Self-Esteem

Self-esteem is an aspect of the way we view ourselves. It's a little different from self-image, which might describe a whole range of characteristics—such as, "I'm American," or "I'm Canadian," or "I am a female"—but without implying whether they are good or bad.

Self-esteem refers to the overall opinion we have of ourselves and the value we place on ourselves as people. Low self-esteem means that the tone of this opinion is negative: for example, "I'm unlovable" or "I'm useless." Of course, most of us have mixed opinions of ourselves, but if your overall opinion is that you are an inadequate or inferior person if you feel that you have no true worth and are not entitled to the good things in life, this means your self-esteem is low.

Low self-esteem can have a painful and damaging effect, personally and especially in your real estate business. At the heart of your self-esteem are your core beliefs about the kind of person you are. If you have low self-esteem, these beliefs will be mainly negative, and negative beliefs are expressed in many ways. In your thoughts about yourself, you're likely to be self-critical, self-blaming, self-doubting, and focus on your weaknesses rather than your positive qualities. The beliefs will affect your behaviour: you may avoid challenges and opportunities, be continually apologetic, or find it difficult to be assertive. They can have an impact on your emotions, generating sadness, guilt, shame, frustration, or anger. This might be reflected in your physical state, making you feel fatigued or tense.

"Many people who are imprisoned in a negative self-image, with low self-esteem, do not attempt much because they do not see themselves worthy of accomplishing much." – Cliff Baird, PhD

Such beliefs can influence many aspects of your real estate business:

• You may feel unworthy when a prospect tells you "No;" therefore, you stop making calls for the day, or even for the week. Go back and review the chapter on letting go of the stories you create in your mind.

• In your personal relationships, you may suffer from terrible self-consciousness, oversensitivity to criticism or disapproval, or excessive eagerness to please. Some people with low self-esteem are prone to be codependent, and they try to always be in control or always put others first, thinking that if they don't, no one will want to know them.

Crucial experiences, which help to form our beliefs about ourselves, often, although not always, occur early in life. What you saw, heard, and experienced in childhood — in your family and at school — will have influenced the way you see yourself.

Examples of early experiences that could lead to your thinking badly of yourself, include:

• systematic punishment, neglect, or abuse

• failing to meet parental standards

• failing to meet peer-group standards

• being on the receiving end of other people's stress or distress

• belonging to a family or social group that other people are prejudiced towards

• an absence of praise, warmth, affection, or interest

• being the odd one out at home or at school

Sometimes negative beliefs about yourself are caused by experiences later in life, such as underachievement, abusive relationships, persistent stress or hardship, or traumatic events.

Past Programming

Since you were conditioned by these negative beliefs while you were younger, you then carry them with you as an adult — into your real estate business. No matter how many courses you take, to call another FSBO (For Sale By Owner) or contact someone from your database, without understanding the destructive power of these beliefs, you will continue to produce the same results in your real estate business, year after year after year. If you don't have a breakthrough with these emotional terrorists, you will always wonder why your production is not growing or not moving as fast as you would like it to. It is because these beliefs have you trapped in a disastrous failure cycle. During my one-on-one coaching sessions with real estate agents, one of the exercises that I make sure I have them go through is to identify what their limiting beliefs are, and I have them write them all out on a piece of paper. Once they complete step one, step two really shows them the impact that a particular belief has had on their personal and business life. Step three is to have them realize the tremendous benefit that would happen when they have a breakthrough. It is amazing to see my clients go through this exercise, and then, on our next weekly coaching call, they will share with me a remarkable victory: a triumph over their past. They could now see a future —abundant with success.

From a Poor Self-Image to Taking Her First FSBO Listing

This reminds me of a coaching client of mine. Being in her early 20s, my client was terrified to call FSBOs because of what the FSBO might say to her. She was agonizing about herself (self-image), and the false assumptions she would say out loud about herself. She gave me many reasons why calling FSBOs was a terrifying idea and how much she did everything to avoid calling them. One day, during our coaching session together, we worked on her mindset in the way she was thinking about FSBOs. I took her through various mindset exercises, and she finally realized that the fear she had was being created by her own mind. Once she acknowledged that she began making phone calls to FSBOs, and then she started booking previews to go and meet with them at their homes. On the first FSBO, my client was nervous and fearful, which is normal; however, she took the action anyway and knocked on the door she had booked with the preview. After a lengthy conversation in the FSBO's home, my client left their home and felt confident. On our next call, my client told me that the FSBO wanted to meet with her again to discuss the possibility of listing their home with her. The next day, my client met with the homeowner, and she took the listing!! She called me with so much excitement. Here is what she said ... "John! Guess what!? I took the listing on my first FSBO appointment!"

I was so happy for her; I had a smile from ear to ear. About a week later, she got the home sold, and she earned $6,800! Isn't it amazing when you can shift the beliefs, which had once held you back, and now set yourself free? I am very proud of her, as she now calls FSBOs with confidence and ease. In fact, she is having so much fun that she just continuously books appointments with FSBOs, takes listings, and earns more money doing the things she loves to do.

FREE BONUS

If you would like to receive a powerful FSBO script, which you can use to confidently speak with FSBOs, please go to *TheBookUnleashed*.com, right now, under Free Bonuses, to receive your free copy today.

READ THIS CAREFULLY

As we grow up, we take the voices of people with us, especially the people who were significant to us. We may criticize ourselves in their sharp tones and make the same comparisons with other people that they did. Our experiences create a foundation for general conclusions about ourselves — judgements about ourselves as people. We can call these conclusions our self-image.

When you find yourself facing situations that bring your self-image into consideration, you will tend to make negative predictions, thinking about your personal and business inadequacy, and all the things that could go wrong.

These negative predictions can especially affect your behaviour in your real estate business in a number of ways:

- They can lead to call avoidance.

- They can lead to unnecessary precautions.

- They can disrupt your performance while prospecting.

- They can lead to success being discounted.

The Cure for a Negative Self-Image and Low Self-Esteem

The self-image hangs like an oil painting in our minds, and we are constantly viewing it and being reminded of how it was created. If, in fact, this portrait is the accumulation of the issues we had to process in childhood and beyond, then we need to change the portrait. WE NEED A NEW OIL PAINTING. Each stroke of the brush needs to be replaced.

With what?

There is only ONE THING every person needs to get through each day and each problem and to live life to the fullest ... just one thing ... GENUINE ENCOURAGEMENT. We need to be with people who encourage us. So, how can we get genuine encouragement consistently? Can we ask for it? Of course, however, it will not satisfy us because we had to ask for it. So, how, then can we get it?

There is a sacred truth found in all faiths and in life experience itself: GIVE, AND IT WILL BE GIVEN TO YOU ... 10-FOLD!

We are familiar with this as the Law of Give and Receive. Whatever you give, you will receive. WE NEED TO BE CAREFUL WITH THE "WHATEVER."

If you give love, you get love, but if you give anger, you get anger. In the case of someone who is imprisoned inside a negative self-image, they need encouragement. YES, at a time when they least feel like it, they must be the source of encouragement to others. The Law really teaches us that whatever we need the most, we should give it away in abundance. We need encouragement, so give it away as often as possible to as many people as possible.

HANG A NEW SELF-IMAGE OIL PAINTING IN YOUR MIND

If you want to overcome a negative self-image and low self-esteem, then you must take the focus off yourself and spend time giving everyone else in your life what you need ... ENCOURAGEMENT ... and you will be sowing the seeds of a very positive, amazing future.

"No one can make you feel inferior without your consent." -Eleanor Roosevelt

Your vision of who you want to be is your greatest asset. If you only do what you can do, you will never be more than you are now. Scott Adams, the creator of the famous comic series, *Dilbert*, attributes his success to the use of positive affirmations. Fifteen times each day, he wrote this sentence on a piece of paper: "I, Scott Adams, will become a syndicated cartoonist." The process of writing this 15 times a day buried this idea deep into his subconscious, putting Adams' conscious mind on a treasure hunt for what he sought. The more he wrote, the more he could see opportunities that used to be invisible to him. And shortly thereafter, he became a highly famous, syndicated cartoonist.

This is but one isolated illustration of the power of the subconscious mind. We are always moving in the direction of our thoughts.

Thoughts are things. They come before everything. Nothing in this world has ever been created without first having the thought ... including getting a cup of coffee or creating a world-famous cartoon.

"Create the highest, grandest vision possible for your life, because you become what you believe." – Oprah Winfrey

Six Ways to Create Healthy Thoughts Towards Yourself to Increase Your Sales:

1. Decide – First, ask yourself, what is important about creating healthy and supportive thoughts towards yourself to grow your business? Write this out.

2. Say Nice Things – Start saying nice things about yourself, such as, "Great job!" "Well done!" "I am proud of me!"

3. Good Enough – Think back to a time when you did something extraordinary, you accomplished something, or you felt proud and worthy about something. What was that? Think about that, and write it out to get present to that moment again. You will notice that you are more than good enough, just as you are. The more you practice this, the higher your self-esteem and confidence will get.

4. Practice Being Kind and Gentle – When things don't go as well as you would like them to, stop focusing on what has gone wrong, but rather focus on who you are. Then, focus on the next step to find the solution. For example, if you submitted an offer and it didn't get accepted, or you didn't get that listing signed or you didn't close on the phone while prospecting, etc., let go of beating yourself up, and just practice being kind and gentle, because YOU ARE ALREADY MORE THAN GOOD ENOUGH. Yes, YOU ARE.

5. Acknowledge Yourself – Acknowledge yourself for the small wins and successes you have had in your personal and businesslife. Do this daily to build up your self-worth and self-esteem. Keep collecting and celebrating these victories. For example, I usually take myself to a nice restaurant and enjoy the moment, appreciating what I have accomplished.

6. Meditation and Yoga – Without a doubt, the combination of yoga and meditation have helped me quiet my mind. It has also allowed me to be kind and gentle with myself, because I took the time to focus on me. This allowed me to respect myself first, which allowed me to see myself at a higher level in my mind.

Five Actions to Abolish a Negative Self-Image and Create an Empowering Mindset:

1. Acknowledge Your WINS in Your Life

Every one of us has some sort of winning in our lives, which we feel proud about: things such as winning our first sports game or scoring our first goal, driving for the first time, selling our first home, receiving our first award.

2. Create and Review Your Evidence of Success Board

Now that you have what you are most proud about in your life, post these, at your home or office, and get your mind to focus and be present with those wins and/or successes in your life. Some clients of mine post their first FSBO listing they took, or their first five Expired Listings they took. By reviewing these daily, it reminds them how good enough they already are.

3. Chant Out Your Affirmations Daily

Below are some affirmations. My suggestion is that you select 3 to 4 maximum affirmations that you can believe and feel good about yourself for. The best way is to stand up and move your body, while allowing yourself to breathe, wearing a big smile on your face.

4. Be Thankful

You are going to see this a lot in this book because it is one of the most powerful things you can get your mind to focus on. Think about 4–5 things you can be most thankful or grateful for in your life. Are you thankful for the amazing health and body you have? Are you grateful to live in this amazing country you are in? Or how about being thankful for the amazing family or children you have? Whichever you select, get present to that daily, and focus your thoughts on that. It works when you work it.

5. Practice Being Kind to Yourself

Again, make sure you say soft, gentle words to yourself, such as, "I am already more than good enough;" "I am already successful;" "I love myself." The more you repeat these throughout the day, and take small simple actions towards what you want, you will feel much better about yourself and what you do.

"Let go of who you think you are supposed to be and be who you are."
– Irene Brown

Because of this need for harmony in our thoughts, we will constantly seek information and proof from our circumstances, to confirm what we have come to believe about ourselves. We will then disregard other evidence to the contrary. If you are always saying to yourself, "I am an idiot," even though you might do other creative things, you will laser your focus on the small mistakes you make (e.g., locking your keys in the car) to validate that you are, in fact, an idiot. You will obsess about those things because they harmonize with what you, your inner voice, say to yourself. To break this programmed inclination, you have to first make the conscious effort to say something positive to yourself and then aggressively search for the authenticating evidence. When you hear your fault-finder voice saying, "I am an idiot," instantly replace the statement with something you know is true. The more you fight, the less the voice will haunt you.

"If you ever lose love, don't go out looking for it. Reach inside you and recreate what you think you lost. You are love. You can't lose you." – Unknown

FREE BONUS

To receive powerful affirmations, which have helped me and my clients conquer a negative self-image, feel worthy, and confidently charge into the marketplace, then go to TheBookUnleashed.com,

right now, under the Free Bonuses tab, opt-in to receive your powerful affirmations.

The Next Chapter

This was a passionate chapter for me to write, given my struggle with low self-worth early on in life. However, by using the tools and strategies in this chapter, it has helped me to grow my businesses to great levels of success, and I know it can work for you too, with daily practice. Practice is the key.

Now that you are being kind and gentle with yourself after reading this chapter, next, I will discuss with you how to escape perfectionism and make progress in your business. Go to the next chapter right now, and I will share with you how you can escape perfectionism and grow your business today.

John Toublaris

Born in Toronto, Canada, John Toublaris is an international speaker, award-winning author, real estate sales and mindset coach. With over twenty-one years of personal development work and professional sales training, John brings a wealth of real estate sales and coaching experience to his practice.

John is well known for and focuses on empowering real estate agents by overcoming individual mindset barriers to achieve greater sales performance. Throughout these years, John has had the privilege to be coached by many world-class real estate coaching and training organizations, which have helped him elevate his performance and quality of life, both personally and in business.

Furthermore, John has surrounded himself with and been trained by Anthony Robbins, Les Brown, Brian Tracy, Bob Proctor, and many other well-known speakers, coaches, and trainers. John is committed to helping his coaching clients achieve top sales achievements to realize their dreams, goals, and desires. John has a clear understanding of the issues and challenges facing individuals seeking to achieve excellence in their life, as he will help you identify your blind spots for greater real estate sales performance and effectiveness in your life.

As an advocate of personal development, self-growth, and sports coaching, John has helped nine different ball hockey teams to win gold medals at the Canada, Ottawa, Montreal, and Toronto Cup Championships, by guiding, empowering, and inspiring his athletes.

John has also been a member of the Canadian National ball hockey team as well. Over the years, John has earned twenty-two medals, in both soccer and hockey, for top performance achievement.

John knows how to win and how to create winning strategies for all those he has the honour to coach.

FARMLAND REAL ESTATE

Albert Lacoursiere

"Buy land, they're not making it anymore" – Mark Twain

When you think of real estate, what comes to mind?

In 2021, when I saw a for sale sign in front of my neighbour's acreage, just down the road from our family farm, I had an idea. I called my dad that evening, as I often call my parents in the evening to chat. I briefly mentioned my idea to him. When his reply wasn't one of disinterest, I continued to explain, and we were soon brainstorming ideas. It was late, and we both decided to sleep on it.

The next day, we had a chat on the phone and agreed to pursue our plan. We contacted the seller and the realtor and made our offer. The seller was happy to deal with us and recalled a memory from 15 years earlier when I lightheartedly mentioned my interest in acquiring the property if she ever decided to sell, as I thought it was a very beautiful and unique place. And here we were.

Our plan was to purchase the acreage, do a bit of work to the house, and develop an area that had never been cleared, then subdivide and sell the house and yard for a price that would cover our initial purchase price in addition to the cost of developing the farmland and repairing the house.

The goal was to end up with 14 more acres of farmland, as it was already attached to our property, and a storage shed for a net cost of zero dollars.

Fast forward a little bit, and our plan changed a bit. We developed the farmland as planned. We use the storage shed that's on site. We did not subdivide and sell the house and yard, but instead, we decided to keep it as accommodations for farm staff. It's a nice yard with a beautiful house and a garage, and it's less than a 20-minute commute from the nearby urban center and only one mile away from the main farm yard. Perfect for somebody wanting that sweet acreage lifestyle.

When I step back to look at the big picture, I see a good investment that evolved into something better by adding value to our main business by using real estate in a creative fashion and by offering value and incentives to my coworkers. Win-win.

Is farmland a good investment? Maybe. Maybe not. I think it is a good investment, but my opinion is quite biased. As long as the human race exists and needs to eat, farmland will be pretty darn important and in very high demand. Macroeconomics 101. Supply and demand. Driving the demand is the continuously growing number of mouths to feed.

On the other side of the equation, the creator isn't making more land. The earth's surface area is finite. Small areas may still be being developed into farmland, but in other areas, farmland area is being reduced by the expansion of urban centers.

Farmland has been the playing field for our family business for nearly a century. It has always been our place of business. At times it has served as the board room where we discuss plans on the fly while we fill the seeder, or where our bankers come out to ride in the harvester in the fall to discuss business while enjoying a day out of the office and learning about our operation. It has been the dining room for many meals, especially during harvest.

How do I determine if farmland is a good investment for me? Well, it depends on what you want to do with it and what you expect from it, as it can serve a different purpose depending on the type of investor you are. For myself, the primary reason for investing in farmland is to, well, farm it.

I am an active investor. As a commercial agriculturalist, my farmland investment doesn't end at the time of acquisition. I reinvest into it every year by growing crops on it.

This requires significant investment every year to pay for equipment, fuel, labour, insurance, professional agronomy and marketing services in addition to other inputs such as seed, fertilizers and crop protection products.

The objective is to invest these inputs into the farmland and gain a larger return at the end of the year. It's a risky game, but it can be very profitable when the stars align.

Crop diversity and healthy agronomic decisions are key, alongside money management, willingness to adapt to change and readiness to make time-sensitive decisions and pivot on a dime, a watchful eye on the markets that change daily, risk management practices, a passion for challenges and a taste for risk.

Oh, and let's not forget to mention mother nature. Actively farming is often used to cash-flow farmland. However, if you are a producer in the process of buying the said farmland using financing, it's unlikely to generate enough returns by itself to make the payment. It may require revenue from multiple pieces of farmland to make the payments for a single piece. This is why it is so difficult to get into farming and for smaller farms to expand.

Our farming operation produces a variety of crops, including wheat, canola, and barley, on a combination of land that is owned and on land that is leased from other landowners, whether they be retired farmers or heirs or relatives who own a piece of this type of real estate. Our operation has also, at times, leased some of our owned lands to others in the area.

Does it make sense to purchase a farm? Maybe if a person bought some land and bought some equipment, then they could start farming. They could do that, but it may not be logical if they don't know exactly what they are doing and have the experience.

Land is costly to begin with, and it would take a lot of planning to determine the equipment needed to get started if they are new to the idea. There have been times when people have bought already operational farms from farmers looking to retire. The farmer stayed at the business as an employee for a predetermined number of years to help with the transition and to teach the new owners the ropes. Alternatively, a farmland investment could be a passive one by purchasing a desirable piece of farmland and leasing it to an active investor, such as a farmer.

Let's jump back to what I said earlier about leasing land from other landowners. The biggest thing about leasing land is relationships. As the land owner, you want good tenants, ones that will take care of the land. The vacancy rate for farmland in my area is basically 0%. Zero. There is usually a lineup of people interested in farming your land.

It is not uncommon for landlord and tenant agreements to last for decades. Agreements can be quite simple. Terms would typically include the duration of the lease, the amount of the lease payments, factors that would affect this number if it's a variable agreement, payment due dates, lease renewal dates, the inclusion of any useable structures etc. There may also be clauses such as the last right of refusal where the tenant may have the first option to renew the lease and sometimes even the first option to purchase the property if the owner considered selling.

So let's say that you acquired a piece of farmland either by inheritance or as an investment. What does ownership look like, and what are some of the basic types of lease agreements that could be considered when negotiating with potential tenants? The ownership part can be as simple as collecting a lease payment once per year and paying the municipal tax once per year, which in many cases is a tax-deductible income expense, but talk to your accountant.

Let's quickly go over some basic types of lease agreements that are sometimes used.

Cash agreement. This is as simple and straightforward as it can get. So many acres at a price of so many dollars per acre.

Crop share agreement. This type of lease agreement is almost like a joint venture and can require a certain level of risk, and the outcome can be a reflection of this, for the better or for the worse. In this situation, the land owner and the tenant would determine a percentage to use as a reasonable investment by each party to cover the cost of the crop. For this example, we will use 25 percent. In some situations, the land owner might provide the piece of land and also pay the tenant for a certain percentage of the input costs to grow a crop, such as 10 percent. After the crop is harvested, the land owner receives a 25 percent share of the production. These values can be negotiated, and every situation will be different. This type of agreement requires a solid relationship between the parties and excellent communication.

Hybrid or variable agreement. This is similar to a cash agreement where a certain price per acre is determined. However, other clauses may be set up, such as bonus payments to the landowner should the crop exceed a certain production target or yield and/or commodity prices reach a certain value.

When determining appropriate lease agreements, it's not usually as straightforward as calculating a figure based on the monetary value of the land, but often based on many variables such as the quality of the land, accessibility, competitive rents in the area, foreseeable input expenses, anticipated production returns, any amenities that come with the land such as storage facilities, and also competitive rents in the area. Again, relationships are the primary factor.

I'm a curious creature, and my curiosity had me recently comparing Canada's historical farmland values to the price of gold, two of our civilization's most valuable asset classes. The data from a recent Farm Credit Canada survey reports that the average national annual change in farmland values in Canada as a whole from 1985 to 2021 was an increase of approximately 5.04%.

A quick internet search brought me to a site where I saw that the average annual gold closing price change for the same period was 5.93%. The 20-year period from 2002 inclusive to 2021 saw average Canadian farmland and gold value changes of +8.96% and +10.98%, respectively. Looking at details, in 2021, Ontario led the eastern provinces in terms of value increase with 22.2% and British Columbia in the west with 18.1% increase.

Alberta's value change was the lowest of the provinces in 2021 at 3.6%. Gold saw a small decrease in value averages of 3.51% from 2020 to 2021 after a massive increase of over 24% from 2019 to 2020. I found interest in doing this random exercise, and my personal conclusion is that I think both assets as investments offer unique and desirable opportunities, such as gold having high liquidity and farmland having the potential for recurring income streams such as rent or production.

I want to recap three possible profit centers of owning or leasing farmland that I mentioned.

Production income can be generated from actively using the land.

Rental income can be passively gained by leasing the land to a producer.

Portfolio income can be created if appreciation develops from holding the asset in demand for the right period of time.

I can honestly say that at the time of writing this piece, I was by no means an expert on the subject of investing in real estate or gold. And now, I am still not an expert! This has simply been my opinion based on my experience in a small area of a very expansive topic, and I hope that you enjoyed reading about it as much as I enjoyed sharing it with you.

Albert Lacoursiere

Albert is a third-generation farmer, a multi-passion entrepreneur, and a father of two. After high school, Albert worked at a farm equipment manufacturer and developed skills in welding and metal manipulation. He later worked for a pipeline company in Alberta. Returning to the family farm in 2004, Albert has committed his time and energy to the operation and has helped develop the business to its current state using a combination of education and experimentation, during which time he studied at Lakeland College in Vermillion, Alberta and obtained a diploma relevant to his profession as a commercial agriculturalist. Many years later, Albert decided for himself that his opportunities to learn and grow are still abundant, and he enjoys investigating a variety of subjects independently, through courses and workshops, and through his network. Family, agriculture, real estate, and personal development are some of his primary focuses.

LUXURY REAL ESTATE

Mira Lulic

I have been in real estate for 13 years. A lot of my sales include higher-end homes.

To sell luxury real estate, you have to create a comprehensive marketing plan that highlights the unique features and benefits of the property to be able to meet your seller's expectations and achieve the desired price.

Some of the marketing techniques I use to market Luxury properties are:

Professional Photography and Videography: Invest in high-quality photography and videography to showcase the property in the best possible light. Hire a professional photographer and videographer who specialize in luxury real estate

Virtual Tours: Create a virtual tour of the property to give potential buyers a 360-degree view of the property. This is especially important if the buyers are from out of town or overseas.

Staging: Staging luxury properties can help to increase their perceived value and ultimately lead to a higher selling price. When done correctly, staging can create an emotional connection between the buyer and the property, which can lead to a quicker sale and a higher price.

Luxury home staging often involves bringing in high-end furniture and decor that complements the style and architecture of the property. The goal is to create a luxurious and welcoming environment that will appeal to potential buyers.

Staging can also help to showcase the unique features of a luxury property, such as a stunning view or a high-end kitchen. By highlighting these features, the property can stand out from other luxury properties on the market and justify a higher selling price.

In addition to physical staging, **virtual staging** can also be effective for luxury properties. This involves using computer-generated images to create a virtual tour of the property, which can help potential buyers envision themselves living in the space.

Market the Lifestyle:

Selling luxury real estate is not just about selling the property but also about selling the lifestyle. Highlight the property's proximity to high-end restaurants, shopping, and entertainment venues.

Host Exclusive Events:

Host exclusive events such as open houses or private showings for potential buyers. This creates a sense of exclusivity and generates interest in the property.

Utilize Social Media:

Use social media platforms such as Instagram and Facebook to promote the property. Hire a social media specialist to create engaging content and target potential buyers.

Partner with Luxury Brands:

Partner with luxury brands such as luxury car dealerships, private jet companies, and high-end jewelry stores to attract affluent buyers.

Develop a strong online presence:

Many buyers start their search online, so it's important to have a website and social media presence that showcases your properties in an appealing way. Use high-quality photos and videos, and highlight the unique features of each property.

Utilize targeted marketing:

Consider using targeted marketing techniques to reach potential buyers who are interested in luxury real estate. This could include targeted ads on social media, email marketing campaigns, or even print advertisements in luxury publications.

Host exclusive events:

Hosting exclusive events can create buzz around your properties and attract potential buyers. Consider hosting a private open house for high-net-worth individuals or hosting an event in partnership with a luxury brand.

Marketing materials:

Luxury open houses may provide high-end marketing materials, such as brochures or videos, that showcase the property in a more professional and polished way. These materials may highlight the unique features and amenities of the property and help to justify the higher asking price.

Offer unique experiences:

Luxury buyers are often looking for unique experiences and amenities. Consider offering things like private tours of the property, access to exclusive events or experiences, or even custom furniture or art installations.

Partner with a luxury real estate agent:

Partnering with an experienced luxury real estate agent who has a strong network of potential buyers can help you sell your properties more quickly and at a higher price point. They can also help you identify the unique selling points of each property and create a targeted marketing strategy.

There are several reasons why someone might choose to sell luxury real estate:

High commissions:

Luxury real estate properties often come with a high price tag, which means that the commission earned by the seller's agent can be significant.

Prestige:

Selling luxury real estate can be a prestigious career choice. It allows you to work with high-net-worth individuals and celebrities and can help to build an agent's reputation as a top performer in the industry. This can lead to more business opportunities in the future.

Potential for growth:

The luxury real estate market is constantly evolving, which means that there is potential for growth and new opportunities.

Creative opportunities:

Selling luxury real estate often requires creativity and innovation. This can be a rewarding challenge for those who enjoy developing unique marketing strategies and finding ways to showcase properties in the best possible light.

Personal satisfaction:

Selling luxury real estate can be a fulfilling career choice for those who enjoy helping others achieve their dreams of owning a high-end property. It can also be rewarding to see the impact that a beautiful home can have on a buyer's life.

Unique properties:

Luxury real estate often includes unique properties that can be exciting to market and sell. These properties may have interesting histories, unique features, or breathtaking views that can make them stand out from other properties on the market.

International appeal:

Luxury real estate often appeals to international buyers, which can open up new markets for real estate agents who are interested in working with buyers from around the world. This can lead to exciting business opportunities and the chance to work with clients from a variety of cultures and backgrounds.

Mira Lulic

I originated from a humble background, having been born and raised in a small Croatian town. I previously owned a business and am currently a successful real estate agent for over 13 years in the Greater Toronto Area (GTA) of Ontario, Canada.

While some may deem it an insignificant detail, I take pleasure in assisting people to find their ideal homes and ensuring that their transitions from one home to another are smooth and dignified. My proficiency in this field has enabled me to achieve remarkable accomplishments. Furthermore, my compassionate and empathetic personality compels me to aid others whenever I can.

Website: www.MiraLulic.com

POWER OF COLLABORATION IN REAL ESTATE

Saurav Sharma

Collaboration is the Key to success in all walks of life. " *Alone we can do so little, together we can do so much.*" This quote by Helen Keller, highlights the importance of working together to achieve great things.

Collaboration brings together diverse perspectives, skills, and knowledge to create innovative solutions and tackle complex challenges. It promotes open communication, trust, and a sense of shared purpose that inspires individuals to work towards a common goal. It is a powerful tool that can lead to tremendous growth and progress. When individuals and organizations come together to share ideas, skills, and resources, they can achieve goals that would be impossible to accomplish alone. Collaboration fosters creativity, improves problem-solving abilities, and promotes a sense of community and shared ownership.

In today's rapidly changing world, collaboration is becoming important as individuals and organizations seek to navigate complex challenges and capitalize on new opportunities. In the real estate industry, things are complex, and this market is constantly changing and evolving, which requires even a higher level of collaboration and teamwork. In this industry, professionals from various backgrounds, including agents, brokers, lenders, developers, architects, law firms, and contractors, must work together to ensure the successful completion of a real estate project.

"The power of collaboration and Team-work cannot be overstated when it comes to Real estate."

One of the most significant benefits of collaboration in real estate is the ability to pool resources and expertise. By working together, different professionals can bring their unique skills and knowledge to the table, allowing for a more comprehensive and effective approach to a project.

Creating the right mindset is one of the best ways to help an individual person become part of the team and contribute to the group dynamic.

Five ways to create a collaborative environment mindset are:

Have a clear mission – the more exciting the mission, the more people will want to be part of the team that contributes to the success of the company.

Define individual and group roles – when people know what's expected of them, they'll work more effectively with less conflict.

Set goals for the team – setting measurable goals makes it easy to measure progress and reduces confusion.

Understand individual strengths and weaknesses – focusing on individual strengths rather than avoiding weaknesses lets people contribute to the team in a winning way.

Emphasize inclusion and cohesion – include people in decision making and set goals and objectives together.

Once a collaborative environment is created, productivity will automatically increase exponentially.

Collaboration takes many forms in the real estate industry; We collaborate with clients to help them through the buying and selling process. We collaborate with builders to obtain services and deliver them to our clients. We collaborate with other agents and brokers to create a win/win situation during a sale. We collaborate with the community to be a positive influence and serve the best.

Questions to ponder as a broker

You already know how to sell houses, but your challenges are more strategic and business related.

1. What's the most effective strategy to get more leads for my agents?

2. What technology will help me best run my brokerage?

3. What CRM Tools should I provide my agents for lead nurturing?

4. What recruiting practices are most effective? How do I differentiate my brand?

Building collaborative networks that are vibrant and mutually beneficial can be a catalyst for positive change and growth when you have the right people on the other end.

Do You Make Team Members Feel Valued?

Do team members perceive that their service on the team is valuable to the organization and their careers? Do they feel that their participation is advancing their career opportunities and bringing positive attention to their contributions?

A double win is accomplished if team members find themselves valued by the organization and also receive ancillary benefits.

These benefits can include growing and developing their skills and career by participating in the team. Making new contacts and, perhaps, finding new mentors who are committed to their growth is a plus, too.

Do you Recognize and Reward Collaborative Team members?

Businesses also need to give team members a way to celebrate the success of their collaborative efforts. One way of doing this is to talk about how the journey started, and it all came together.

Videos, podcasts, and blogs are all great tools for sharing collaboration success stories. It helps to recognize the accomplishments of the group while highlighting the role that each individual made toward the group's success. Celebrations for collaborative efforts and performance rewards are ways that the brokerage can emphasize how important collaborative work is in setting values and driving the business.

Collaboration is the future of Real Estate Marketing.

The ability to share information between colleagues and agents in real time, especially when it comes to listing details and sales data, is invaluable. Collaborating with others can be more productive and creative, innovative, and efficient. Collaboration software should be easy to use with a clear and intuitive interface so that you don't have to spend time learning it and easy to integrate with your contact database and team. A well-designed dashboard is crucial for collaboration success because it allows team members to view real-time information about their tasks or projects at any given moment. The use of a Mobile App is a must -Realtors spend so much time out of the office that logging into a desktop application on the road is impracticable and obsolete.

Thus, Collaboration is the key to success for every real estate marketer. Collaboration leads to better results because everyone involved has something unique to offer the project. It's not just about finding a solution; it's about finding the best solution for everyone involved in the project.

At Exp Realty Intelligence Group, our team comes from diverse backgrounds, and with their enriching experience, we have a mixed bag of expertise in our team, e.g. from Sales and Marketing experts, Pre-Construction Specialist, IT professionals, seasoned entrepreneurs, people from a media background, Property Management, Mortgage specialists, Accounting, Engineers, Business Development and Sports. When these professionals work together, they create a more effective and efficient process that maximizes their collective strengths. Collaboration and networking with real estate professionals and expertise provide good advice, experience, and learning patterns too.

Collaborative Teamwork Equals Teamwork and Collaboration

Collaboration is another hot topic today - most people assume that collaboration is simply another way of saying teamwork. But the difference between the two is not just a matter of semantics.

Teamwork is the combined action of people working toward the same end goal. When people talk about teamwork, they mean more than just completing a task; it conveys the work that comes from teams working together effectively. The strength of a team comes from supporting each other, communicating well, and doing your share.

A collaborative team is a slightly different version of a traditional team because its members have different skill sets. Although the members have varying areas of expertise, they share similar goals, resources, and leadership.

Importance of Team Collaboration in the workplace :

- Team Collaboration Promotes Problem-Solving
- Collaboration Drives Innovation
- Team Collaboration Breakd Down Barriers
- Team Collaboration Builds Better Communication
- Collaboration Makes Team Members Consider a Bigger Picture
- Collaboration Encourages Knowledge Sharing
- Team Collaboration Boosts overall team happiness.
- Increases Jobs Satisfaction and Employee Retention

Collaborative leaders can span the scope of your business by engaging people outside of their direct control and getting them to work as a team with a common goal. When businesses talk about collaborative leadership, they mean distributed organizational structures that are either cross-unit, cross-functional or cross-organization. These groups get employees at all levels with a stake in the outcome. This strategy is more about facilitating the group effort than about making decisions for the group. In other words, a collaborative leader leads the group's process, not the group itself.

A big part of collaboration is Coordination. Coordination is about achieving efficiency and about telling participants how and when they must act. This concept is similar to collaboration and teamwork because its goals are the same.

Of course, Cooperation is an integral element of teamwork, collaboration, and coordination. Cooperation usually consists of two or more people sharing ideas or activities. You often share the information you generate from cooperation - while it is sometimes required, it is an informal process. Compared with teamwork, collaboration, and coordination, cooperation is the activity that requires the least amount of shared purpose and dependence on team members.

Communication is another key element of working together. It is a well-mannered approach to the workplace, requiring all members to talk to each other. It involves interacting in whatever way works best for you and your team personality and relationship-wise.

Even though these five terms have similar connotations, they differ in their level of purpose and dependence.

PURPOSE DEPENDENCE →

COMMUNICATION → COOPERATION → COORDINATION → TEAMWORK → COLLABORATION

The types of collaboration skills

Communication skills,

Emotional intelligence, and

Respect for diversity.

1. Collaboration And Communication

Communication refers to how people send out and receive messages. This critical skill involves nonverbal cues, including active listening, managing yourself in the moment, and being able to understand yourself and others. Often considered a soft skill, communication is vital because it is the soul of your business. Good communication is at the center of everything successful you do within your company. A good communicator conveys their point in a simple and clear manner, people understand their message, and the work gets done.

Relate their message to their listener on a personal level

Always provide factual information

Give specific information in a brief manner

Ask questions to ensure understanding

Ask questions for clarification

Listen actively

2. Emotional intelligence

Emotional intelligence is a skill that helps you sense your emotions and manage them, but also quickly identify how others are feeling at the moment.

Show more empathy and compassion towards your teammates.

Practice objectivity and transparency in communication.

Don't get offended easily.

Avoid taking criticism personally.

Pay close attention to the verbal and non-verbal cues of your teammates.

Show resilience.

3. Respect for diversity

If you're working in a multicultural team, cultivating diversity should be high on your list of workplace priorities.

Collaboration thrives in the work setting that encompasses:

Communicating openly,

Being sensitive to ethnic and religious backgrounds,

Establishing consensus,

Promoting group discussions, and

Cultivating an environment where every team member can share their opinions. By nurturing these three types of skills, you and your colleagues will feel more comfortable working with each other.

Commitment to success!

Commitment to success is the final pillar that allows teams to collaborate well in the workplace. If everyone on your team is strongly committed to success, you'll find that collaboration is easy to foster and that overall efficiency will improve and shine.

CONCLUSION

Working in teams can have tremendous benefits in the workplace. Collaboration is when two or more people come together and share their ideas to create a common goal. Working together helps people to feel more connected and part of a larger team, as well as helps to generate innovative and efficient solutions. New technologies allow us to collaborate with colleagues regardless of distance, meaning an increasingly global perspective on workplace events. Working in a team environment can tremendously benefit uncovering each employee's unique skills and expertise. When colleagues work together, they are inspired to think outside the box, explore creative solutions, and draw strength from one another. This access to out-of-the-box thinking and problem-solving leads to exciting growth opportunities for employees and the company.

Unlocking the potential of each employee is invaluable for any business. When you allow individuals to work collaboratively, their hidden talents often emerge, which can benefit everyone within the organization. Offering collaborative projects gives teams a chance to discover unexpected depths among themselves while simultaneously providing an enriching work experience that boosts morale and productivity. In today's interconnected world, collaboration is more important than ever, and those who can master it will definitely thrive in any field. As they say, "**Alone we're a small flame, and together we're ONE BIG FIRE.**"

Saurav Sharma

Saurav Sharma is a Seasoned Entrepreneur, Sales Leader, International Best-Selling Co-Author, Marketer, Investor, Ex-banker, a Real Estate Enthusiast. He is currently serving as the Director of Business Development at Realty Intelligence Group, a leading Real Estate Firm based in Toronto, Canada. With Over 20 years of Professional Experience, Saurav has gained vast exposure and a wealth of knowledge in the Investing, Mortgage Industry, Banking and Finance, and Negotiations, making him a highly sought-after real estate professional.

Saurav's holistic approach to "Intelligent Advisory" is based on numbers and statistics, where he believes that "there is no substitute for the facts." His mission is to provide his clients with cost-effective real estate solutions while maintaining the utmost standards of integrity and professionalism. He and his Team of Expert Advisors go above and beyond to ensure that his clients' real estate experience exceeds their expectations, and his unparalleled determination and diligence have helped him establish a stellar reputation within the industry.

Saurav's diverse professional background and extensive experience have equipped him with a unique perspective on the Real Estate industry, making him a trusted advisor to his clients. He is committed to delivering results and creating long-lasting relationships built on trust, respect, and transparency.

Saurav@sauravsharma.ca

www.realtyintelligencegroup.com

Gut Feeling in Real Estate

Sigi Scholten

The Importance of your Gut Feeling and your Inner Voice when buying an Investment Property

So, you have settled into your professional life and want to work smart and not always hard? You have started to invest in a financial portfolio, but you want to generate a secondary income and have heard that real estate is the best investment down the road. Where do you start, and how should you decide what is the best option?

When it comes to deciding, the brain considers facts and is striving to make the best objective decision. One's intuition, though, might tell a different story, and you should not just dismiss it.

Your gut feeling comes in and helps inform our decision-making process when faced with an important decision.

People always have a gut feeling when making decisions. This innate response can be wrong and can lead one astray from rational action, but it can also be correct.

After thoroughly understanding the facts of your situation and discussing them with others, you may decide on a course of action that makes sense to all parties involved in the transaction.

Listen to your gut, however, before signing on the dotted line and be sure this falls within your comfortable risk tolerance level.

A woman had an uneasy feeling about buying a 4-unit investment property, but her realtor helped her check all the technical facts, and the bank ran the numbers and advised her to go ahead with the purchase as it was considered a good investment. Six months later, tenants started complaining about breathing problems and moved out one after the other, it was hard to find new tenants which then also left, and 13 months after closing a contractor discovered that there was mould behind the walls impacting tenant's health. She could not prove that it was pre-existing and not her responsibility, so she had to make repairs without rental income for an extended time. She maxed out her mortgage and eventually had to sell at undervalue, which was devastating for her finances.

A man found out that a new developer was offering pre-construction investments of stacked townhouses in a medium-sized town where there had been no example of it before. This investor saw the project and was drawn to it. The finances were sound, but the location wasn't ideal, yet it was walkable to the city center.

Nothing was known about the developer in town; could he be trusted? Would this rent well? After trying to gather as much information as possible, he consulted his gut feeling, which told him that it was a risk worth taking.

During the time of construction, the real estate market changed, re-sale prices went up, and more and more people investigated smaller and more affordable rentals. This investor was so lucky to sell his house after 2.5 years for almost double the price.

As mentioned, the legwork comes first. When it comes to numbers, there are three different ways to approach the question of whether an investment is sound, and you should look into all three of them:

a.   **The Income Approach**

Sum up the yearly income (rents times 12) and deduct the costs to arrive at the yearly net income. Examples of those costs are property taxes, insurance costs, maintenance costs, costs for potential vacancies and property management. Take utilities only into consideration if paid by the landlord. After subtraction, you will arrive at the net rental income. Research what is considered a good return on investment rate – the interest rate that the real estate investment brings in relation to the capital invested. In our current market, that might be a number between 4 and 5 %. Divide the net income by this percentage, e.g., a net income of $40,000 annually / 0.05 = $800,000

This means that an investment project that brings in $40,000 should have a price of $800,000 or less so that an investor realizes their income goal.

b.   The Appreciation Approach

Find out what the overall appreciation rate (the percentage prices for real estate properties are rising) in a real estate market has been in the past 10-15 years and find a trend, e.g., prices have risen by 3 % annually over the years in the market.

Dive deeper into the neighbourhood development of prices where the object is that you are looking at and compare that appreciation rate to the overall market. If it is at the same rate or higher, it is positive.

c.   The Rule of Thumb Approach

The rent you can generate with a property in 10 years should at least be 50% of the price or more. This rule is just a quick check to verify the results of a. and b.

With real estate usually being a significant investment, it is important to do your extensive homework as described before taking the plunge. How do you now take the plunge?

Use the following simple steps and use your gut instinct to make a sound decision:

1.   Admit to yourself that you have formed an opinion even before you are looking into the facts and weigh in on them – this realization will help you to be more open about options.If several people around you tell you that a townhouse is a bad investment, you might not be open to an opportunity like that.

2.   Gather facts for all alternatives, including comparables, location and rentability, and dollar amount. Find five relevant factors for the project and establish a pro and con list.

If you are looking to buy a legal duplex and have a few listings in different neighbourhoods in town, research as much about the properties as you can, establish the factors you have decided on, arrange for showings with a realtor and take notes when you tour the houses in person, that you have analyzed before in your abc evaluation.

3.   Back home, create a scoring system so that you can allocate points from 1-5 for each factor per alternative and, rate them, run the numbers. As different factors can have different priorities, choose the three alternative projects that score high and make sense.

4.   Take the position of a fly on the wall so that you can see the facts from the outside and imagine you must advise a third person on it.

5.   Take a break; best if it is overnight. The next day, start the day with a morning routine and sit down one more time. Look at the three chosen alternatives and read through them one more time after you have had a good cup of tea or coffee. Listen to yourself. Imagine yourself back at the properties and recreate how it felt.

Don't try to rationalize at that point; let your gut feeling evaluate those three best alternatives. It could tell you to favour one that does not have the top score, but that is alright as different factors could have a different priority.

6.   Decide, and don't second-guess yourself. Make the decision and run with it. If you have done all the legwork, your decision will be sound and will pay off. Discover, evaluate, calculate, feel and be brave! Build a sound real estate portfolio step by step. Let it unfold and watch it for a certain time (e.g., for 2-4 years) before you can leverage the capital you have built in our property and add to your portfolio in buying

the next property – how to do that is a process that I am happy to share another time.

Any questions? Contact me at sigi@sigischolten.ca, and I will be happy to share my wisdom.

Sigi Scholten

Living life, loving life and investing smart

Sigi is a modern-day jack-of-all-trades. A traveller and culture enthusiast, she has called four countries home and experienced countless cultures of the world.

She came to Canada in 2011 and has built her future and wealth since then.

A Mom of two amazing kids, wife of an amazing man and engineer. She is a cooking enthusiast, teacher, HR specialist, real estate broker @eXp Realty and team lead with her work partner at TEAMHOMEWORK in Kingston, Ontario.

She feels attracted to nature and water and the beauty of Ontario!

Sigi has been licensed in Real Estate since 2014 and has served on the Board of Directors for the Kingston Real Estate Board for two terms and as the Chair of the Government Relations Committee.

Sigi has helped numerous clients acquire real estate, coached how to invest wisely and how to build a real estate portfolio and a secondary income that rocks!

Her motto is: Living life one day at a time!

sigi@sigischolten.ca

THE REVERSE MORTGAGE SOLUTION

Diana Francis

One of my most frequent requests is to explain a Reverse Mortgage. What it is, How it works, and How it's different from a traditional mortgage. Put plainly, a Reverse Mortgage is a mortgage.

While there are a few key differences between conventional and reverse mortgages, they're both mortgages. The differences are about when you qualify for a Reverse Mortgage, how much you can borrow, how you borrow it, and how you repay it.

I use the example of Alison, a 65-year-old retired Restaurant Manager and Barry, a 67-year-old retired Construction Contractor. Neither has a pension plan, although both have some retirement savings.

They have a home they spent 30 years sweating and working hard to pay off their conventional mortgage on a house now worth about $700,000. They also have two children off at College and are concerned about Barry's elder sister, with health issues. They've been considering renovating so Barry's sister can stay with them.

They want to continue to help their children complete their schooling. They'd also like to do some travelling. The renovations and University costs are pretty substantial, so they've considered taking a Reverse Mortgage.

Alison has been looking at the requirements for a Reverse Mortgage to see if she and Barry qualify. They're both 55+, the minimum age to qualify for a Reverse Mortgage. Their property taxes are up to date. Their home is debt free and worth considerably more than the minimum value of 250 thousand dollars needed to qualify. And they've maintained their home over the years, so it's in good condition.

Alison also dispelled several myths about Reverse Mortgages during her research. She discovered that you still own your home with a Reverse Mortgage, which the lender does not, just like a traditional mortgage. Their names remain on the Title until the property gets sold or after they're both gone. She discovered. Reverse Mortgages have a no negative equity guarantee, meaning the amount they would owe would not exceed the fair market value of their home.

She found Reverse Mortgages were not more expensive. Having the property appraised, having a lawyer review the paperwork, and paying closing costs and administration fees were similar to when they first bought their home. She did find that the interest rates on a Reverse Mortgage can be higher than a traditional mortgage, but that was more than offset by not having to make regular, ongoing monthly mortgage payments on their lower, fixed retirement income.

And the Reverse Mortgage interest rates were still lower than the quote they received for a Line of Credit or Fixed term loan from their bank. And both the line of Credit and the fixed-term loans required monthly repayment plans.

Alison told Barry what she had found, and they began looking at how to use a Reverse Mortgage. They would need a substantial amount to complete the renovations for Barry's sister.

They could also use a smaller monthly payout. This payout would initially help their children with their College expenses, then transition to helping pay for in-home health care costs as Barry's sister ages and her health issues become more complex.

Finally, and most importantly in Barry's eyes, they could go on that trip Alison has been discussing since they started dating; one of her bucket list items that Barry felt determined his wife would have. A Reverse Mortgage would give them all three outcomes. Alison and Barry looked at the details, the advantages and disadvantages, and decided to approach a mortgage professional about getting a Reverse Mortgage.

After gathering their financial details and having the house appraised, Alison and Barry applied for and received a Reverse mortgage. They could have received 55% of the value of their home but opted for 40%. They'll use half to renovate a suite for Barry's sister and a future caregiver. The other half they will take in monthly payments over the next seven years to help with both College expenses and caregiver costs.

It is now three years since they took out their Reverse Mortgage. The renovations are complete, and Barry's sister is happy in her suite, living independently with minimal assistance for the first two years and having a caregiver assisting her for the past year.

They've attended graduation ceremonies for their children and are the proud parents of a newly minted doctor and architect. The monthly payments have gone from paying University living expenses to paying for caregiver services.

They took the trip Alison always wanted to, plus a couple more. Alison added more destinations to her bucket list. Barry started his bucket list.

They've just celebrated Barry's 75th birthday. He was sad as it was his first since his sister passed away but happy having his grandchildren there.

Barry still tinkers in the garage and volunteers his expertise with Habitat for Humanity. Alison volunteers at the local food bank and teaches cooking classes.

He and Alison had recently decided to rent out the renovated suite and just took on a tenant. They're updating their bucket lists now that they have additional income from the rental.

Twenty years have passed since Alison and Barry took out the Reverse Mortgage that changed the trajectory of their lives. It gave Barry's sister a good quality of life during her final years; it helped their children find career success, and it helped them see parts of the world they could only imagine visiting previously. But, mostly, it eliminated their financial stress and allowed them to grow old 'gracefully' and on their terms.

Alison has just said goodbye to Barry. At 87, after a long and bountiful life, Barry passed on. Alison will stay in their home for another four years until she reaches 89. After that, and will travel more, this time showing parts of the world to her grandchildren. She will be there while they grow, the doting grandmother.

With her health deteriorating for several months, Alison decides to go into a long-term care residence with medical facilities to make her final years as pleasant and comfortable as possible. She and her children find a wonderful home where she will have friends and activities and be happy in the last days of her life. In addition, there was no worry about the costs of the care home. With the Reverse Mortgage combined with their modest savings, Alison found she could be picky about the care residence she lived in, not having to worry about cost or adding any financial burden to her children.

Their home had continued to increase in value over the years slowly, so when Alison moved into long-term care, a discussion with her children over the future of the family home ensued. First, Alison could repay the Reverse Mortgage and gift the house to either or both of her children since there's still equity in the home. Then, she could sell the home. Alison's equity means after repaying the Reverse

Mortgage; she can still leave a healthy College fund for each of her grandchildren.

Alison and Barry realized their dreams, helped their children and grandchildren know theirs and cared for Barry's sister. All this through prudent planning and leveraging the equity they had in their home with a Reverse Mortgage solution.

Diana Francis

International Bestselling Co-Author in the book Self-Empowerment RESET.

She's your guide to building wealth through investment in real estate. Whether you're buying your first home, a second property, or investment property, she will ensure you get the best mortgage for you! Mortgage financing doesn't have to be difficult; let her walk you through the process.

As your independent mortgage professional, she will be happy to provide you with mortgage options. She will assess your financial situation, listen to your goals, and suggest mortgage products that help get you there. It would be her pleasure to work with you.

Also, she is the founder of *Living my Dreams* and a new Non-Profit initiative *FEED Now – For Education & Empowerment Development Now*. She is committed and dedicated to helping others achieve their dreams and empowering her community, and enthusiastic in developing tools for them to use in the achievement of their outcomes.

She is on a mission to help people live their dreams. Because for too long, she didn't live hers.

Diana Francis

Mortgage Agent

diana@porchlightmortgages.com

porchlightmortgages.com

LIFE AS A REAL ESTATE AGENT IN SOUTH AFRICA

Juanita Kapp

Life as a Real Estate Agent has been quite the adventure! Not only do I love working with the diverse individuals that I meet, but the thrill of a successful sale is simply unmatched.

I started working in the Real Estate sector in 2009. At that time, South Africa was almost at the end of its recession, but the negative impact that this crisis inflicted on our country was still clear in the property market. I was determined to flip the script and started my studies with the EAAB (Estate Agency Affairs Board) here in South Africa.

We had quite a few modules to complete and had to write a rigorous test which included questions regarding the legalities that accompany sales and rentals in the property market.

Since then, there have been many different learning curves that have shaped me into the self-confident and skilled agent that I am today. It is definitely a requirement for agents to keep their momentum whilst building up their client base, as one powerful connection can facilitate the generation of many leads, which eventually has the potential to birth one or many sales. I find that resilience is a quality that an agent has to develop and cultivate as our world keeps changing economically.

Many agents that started out in the property market in those years have since moved on to seek greener pastures. I remember that for some of them, being a Real estate agent was simply a hobby or a side hustle, meaning that they weren't always as diligent to bank the amount of hours needed to close a sale.

That having been said, I feel it is necessary to place much focus on how hard Real estate agents actually work whether it be full-time or part-time. There are long days, countless meetings as well as many activities and tasks that are completed behind the scenes. Clients often make arrangements and then end up being either late for the viewing or the listing or cancelling the meeting for another day. Countless phone calls are made during the course of a week. Team building, training, administration and filing is the order of the day. Yet, the hard work and pressing hours make it all worth it in the end!

There are some agents that operate both in sales and property rentals. In my case, I find it easier to stick with one of the two as I believe that proper focus is needed to ensure optimal service and delivery. I am an agent that loves to be involved in the sales arena of the Real Estate market.

My focus is set mainly on residential and commercial sales as I find the industrial and raw land sector to be too wrapped up in proverbial "red tape" due to ever-changing SA laws and regulations. Deals in the industrial and raw land sectors can often take a few months or even years before completion, and a lot can change legally within that space of time.

It is exhilarating to receive a call from a potential client whose property needs to be listed and marketed. For me personally, meeting with these individuals equals an opportunity not only to make a sale but also to form a long-lasting relationship with new connections.

I absolutely adore working directly with homeowners and buyers. Many personalities come to the fore, and it is interesting to note the different group dynamics and thinking patterns between the various families. What is acceptable for one family might not be as alluring for the next. Hence, the Real estate agent definitely has to know how to work with various types of individuals from different cultural backgrounds.

I enjoy the listing process tremendously as it involves taking photos of the property and uploading them on the Real estate company's website. It can be a time-consuming part of the process, but if done correctly, it can benefit both the seller and the agent greatly.

I find that it is important for the agent not only to be knowledgeable about their field and area of expertise but being accommodating and friendly goes a long way. This sets the foundation for a strong working relationship and smooths the road to the successful completion of a sale. Sellers simply want two things: a) They want to sell their property at a market-related price, and b) they want to enjoy the peace of mind that their appointed agent will do everything in his/her power to give the best service possible.

On the flip-side, a buyer wants the same effort from a Real estate agent whilst looking for a comfortable, affordable and beautiful home to call their own.

Often agents have to think in innovative and creative ways to make a deal work. This can be quite exhausting as the process includes not only the seller and the buyer but also the designated representatives at the bank. It is thus not only necessary for the Real estate agent to get along well with the seller/buyer but also to have strong ties with the bank officials. Interest rates have to be negotiated along with the term of payment for the home loan.

On top of that, transfer fees have to be calculated, and bond cancellation fees have to be communicated. To add to this swirly, whirly of negotiation, there are also the services of the conveyancing attorneys, which include loads of personal documentation and accompanying forms that have to be completed and handed in. This sounds like quite a mouthful, and believe me, it is!

Real estate agents can often feel like they are drowning in the list of activities needed for the transactions they are busy with, but the truth of the matter is, once they have the correct system in place, which I like to refer to as my "Roll out schedule," these activities become second nature.

In my opinion, a Real Estate agent has to have strong administration skills. This will prove to be a great advantage for the agent when it comes to working alongside competitive Real estate agencies in their area. Time waits for no one, so the Real estate agent has to be diligent in his/her daily activities. I find that if I carefully plan my week during the course of my weekend, I get most of my tasks done by the end of each designated day.

Following up on the progress of the transaction at each different department proves to be key in getting the deal done in a record amount of time. This can happen in a daily, weekly or even monthly fashion. Daily follow-up calls would, for instance, include contacting the bank and requesting a progress report on the loan application, weekly calls would include contacting the conveyancer's attorneys for updates on their paperwork, and monthly calls would most likely include following up on the registration of the property once the sale reaches that point in the process.

When these calls have been made, it is imperative that all information is relayed immediately to the seller/buyer or both in some cases. This builds their trust in your abilities, and it also displays the agent's level of professionalism. I normally use a texting system when engaging in daily updates, which doesn't interfere with my client's daily tasks but which proves to keep them well-informed.

I cannot place enough focus on the fact that a strong work ethic and determination is what separates successful Real estate agents from the rest of the pack. When surrounding yourself as an agent with a solid and committed team, these qualities automatically transpire.

Another important point is that as a Real estate agent, you will continuously learn new and improved ways to go about your tasks. Make sure to pursue every training opportunity possible, build up your fellow agents at all times and stay humble. As the saying goes, *"Teamwork makes the dream work!"*

I am listing a few pointers on lessons that I have learned over the course of the years. This might assist aspiring or existing agents in discovering the lovely and magic essence of being a Real Estate agent:

- Make sure that you are knowledgeable about a property or topic at hand when dealing with a potential buyer or seller. Nothing scares off an individual faster than inexperience displayed by a Real estate agent! Remember you are working with the most intimate arena of the family life, that is, the family home which represents their place of safety and security.

- If you don't know the answer to a question, simply say, "I am not 100% sure, but I will be sure to find out and let you know immediately."

- If you get stuck during the course of the process of completing a transaction, lean on your fellow agents for assistance and advice.

Always be open to advice and instruction; it will let your team know that you value them, and most importantly, it will teach you a new valuable side of your area of expertise.

- Should the occasion arise that you make a mistake, own it and correct it as fast as possible using the best measure for your client and the other parties involved.

- Believe in yourself at all times. Confidence is a magnet to potential clients both on the buyer and seller side of the fence.

- Always speak highly of your team and fellow Real estate agents. They work just if not even harder than you, and they deserve to have a good reputation.

- Stay humble in all things. Although your success streak proves that you are skilled and equipped, sellers and buyers look to form a personal connection with the Real estate agent and often deter from working with haughty agents. Make it a pleasure for them to work with you. This will prove to be a positive move in the right direction for future business that you want to conduct.

- Live and work with integrity. It is better to do the right thing than to do the wrong thing in order to benefit from others. Integrity speaks for itself, and you will have that peace in your heart when you go to bed at night that you did the right thing. Divine doors will open for you and business will fall in your lap at all times. I speak from experience and I mention this because I want what is best for you.

- Never forget how difficult it was for you to start out, own your journey and help new and upcoming agents wherever you can. It will be worth it in the long run.

- Enjoy life. A positive outlook on life goes a very long way. Make sure to keep your energy vibration high at all times and to brush off the things that want to drag you down ultimately. You've got this! You can do anything you put your mind to! I believe in you!

My final comments would simply be that life is about personal and professional development. The greatest investment that you can ever make is in your own development! Always keep a smile on your face and know that you are worth the time and the effort it takes to make the necessary, uplifting changes you have to make in your life. It will elevate you on a deep and personal level, and your sales in the Real estate market will simply spike. Now let's get out there and conduct more successful sales!

Juanita Kapp

Since she was a young child, she always wanted to "Tame the pen and the sword" and has made it her mission to do just that. She was an ordained Pastor for 15 years and enjoyed working with congregations. She has always been a natural speaker, and worked her way up in various Corporations whilst being in the ministry. In 2020 during the Covid-19 pandemic, she decided to change her life and follow her heart's passion. She became an entrepreneur of note through pure willpower and personal choice. She has since opened various businesses that are highly successful and has started to travel the world. Her newest venture is Meticulous Safaris, which she will be hosting in South Africa to various of the American Leadership groups that she belongs to (AMA, CLA, BLN & Underdog Millionaire Group). She is excited about the future and the developments that it will present. Personal and Professional development has always been at the top of her priority list. Her trip to New Jersey, USA, in January 2023 is a time worth remembering as she had the opportunity to meet all her online business colleagues and business partners. She plans to travel the globe in order to share her energy and positive outlook on life with those who cross her path. As an entrepreneur, she is a risk-taker and will continue to be one. She says, *"The sky is the limit in what we can achieve, if only we would take the courage to believe."*

Founder and Owner of the Meticulous Moments Podcast
Founder & Owner of the Meticulous Martial Arts Mastermind
Co-Founder and Owner of the KAPPTOR Connection
Real Estate Agent at Harcourts

www.meticulousmoments.com

RURAL LIVING IN ONTARIO

Shivana Shamseer

So you want to leave city living behind and move out to the country. Wide open spaces, big blue sky, rolling hills, and your country home! But you've never owned a rural property before. Many of the extra costs that will affect your finances on a day-to-day basis are often over and above the cost of your mortgage payments. They are often costs associated with where your home is located. Then there are just some basics of country living details that you need to know about. Your lifestyle will be greatly affected, so I'd like you to consider what you need to know before making any commitments. Even if you believe you've found the perfect home let's take a look together.

Let's talk water supply! When you live in a rural home, very often, your water comes from a well on your property. Proper well location and construction are key to the safety of your well water (*i.e.*, contamination). There are generally two types of wells that are found, dug wells and drilled wells. A dug well is usually just that, a well dug by shovel or backhoe and lined with stones or brick tiles and are typically 50 feet deep. These wells are generally wide and shallow. Drilled wells are constructed by rotary drilling machines and can be much deeper and access water at greater depths than dug wells, and typically they are around 100-150 feet deep. Generally speaking, drilled wells are preferred where possible as water at a deeper depth, out of the way of rain runoff water, is usually cleaner and less likely to be contaminated. In either case, the cap on your well should always remain in place, so that surface contamination is not a factor in the cleanliness of your well water.

Once your well water is brought into the house, you will need to manage that water before it gets circulated throughout the house.

First, your water will be brought to the surface by a pump and then through a pressure tank. You will then find a way to filter that water. Many homeowners these days are choosing an ultraviolet (UV) light water purification system to remove contaminants from the water. Sometimes an additional filter treatment may also be used.

After water supply consideration, you'll need to understand **septic systems**. What is a septic system anyways? It's an underground and water-tight container made of concrete, polyethylene, or fiberglass. It is a system that collects wastewater from your home, retains the solid material and returns treated effluent water to the soil through a filter bed. Septic systems are often found on rural properties where there is no municipal sewage service.

At a high level, a septic system operates as follows. All of the wastewater from your home runs through a main drain into your septic tank. The solid materials sink to the bottom, and bacteria breaks down these solids. Fats and grease flow to the top. The liquid passes through an effluent filter near the top of your septic tank into a pipe that leads to the filter bed (or drain). Perforated pipes in this filter bed allow treated wastewater to flow into layers of gravel. Bacteria breaks down wastewater through the gravel layers and then into the soil. The soil further removes any impurities. This final treated water then filters through to groundwater. The solid waste remains in the tank and is required to be pumped out.

You can see that the wastewater from the septic tank eventually is treated and flows back into the groundwater. A property that has both a well and a septic tank, is required to have well water drawn from an area away from the septic runoff. There are minimum standards for this distance in each region.

Another thing to consider is whether or not the water from your well is hard water. Hard water is water that has a high mineral content. Hard water is treated by way of a water softener. This is a process of removing minerals like calcium, magnesium and other minerals from drinking water. Hard water tends to leave spots on pots and glasses and scum and scale on appliances and can often lead to high repair bills over time. One thing to watch for is that the discharge from your water softener cycle does not get fed into your septic system. The concern is that the high levels of salt in the discharge from the water softener will kill the bacteria in the tanks that is required for the tank to operate efficiently.

Let me share with you some extra costs to think about when you are considering your perfect country home.

1. The extra costs of heating your home. Many urban properties in urban areas are heated with natural gas, and very rarely is natural gas an option for rural properties. Why? This is because our gas companies likely don't have natural gas lines running alongside those rural roads. Most rural homes are heated with oil or propane. Both of these have to be refilled by a mobile delivery service multiple times throughout the year. Typically this means an annual rental for the holding tank to contain the product, plus delivery fees, plus the costs of the fuel.

2. Your home insurance costs are typically more expensive as there is less likely to be municipal fire hydrants on the streets nearby, which means your fire protection service will be via pumper tank instead. Your proximity to the nearest fire hall will greatly impact your insurance rates. The longer it takes a pumper tank to get to you, the more fire damage will occur.

3. Car insurance also tends to be higher as you are driving more than you were when you were living in the city. This is mainly because you are farther away from everything, like groceries, amenities, schools, parks and recreation and more. There is virtually no public transportation, so owning a vehicle is usually a must.

4. What about pesky rodents? Yes, these creatures can definitely be homewreckers. From field mice, to raccoons and deer, wildlife can be a burden to live with. Field mice can squeeze through the tiniest space and use their teeth to gnaw through just about anywhere and find their way to your kitchen and will find ways to burrow into warm, inviting spaces like your closet for their nesting places. And guess what? These rodents multiply so rapidly that once, they are in, it's hard to control. Keeping them away before they get in is much easier than trying to set traps and catch each and every last one of them. Raccoons are known to try to nest in your roof trusses. Once they find a way in, you'll need to call for a service to trap and release them.

5. The Cost of Living is also something to consider. Your proximity to amenities is often much further and will cost you time and gas. it seems like everything about rural living is more expensive, including wait times for deliveries and services.

6. High-paying job offerings tend to be less available in rural areas or simply just further away.

7. The cost of modern conveniences like cable and internet service can be more expensive than expected. Sometimes there are no cable lines, or very old cable lines, and no high-speed service is available. In this modern work-from-home world, reliable internet service is often a big requirement that is not readily discussed in properties listed for sale. Also, modern ways of living like Uber, grocery delivery, and takeout are also not likely to be available.

8. Access to health care is not always easy; sometimes, living rurally means you could live more than an hour away from a hospital or medical services. If you or your family members require regular medical services, consider that rural living may not be for you.

9. More land sometimes means more problems. If you're a handy person, perhaps you can find it easier to manage some unexpected day-to-day living situations. What if a tree falls upon your driveway? How will you manage? You can't just drag it out of the way or drive over it.

You'll probably have to own a chainsaw or find a neighbour who does, who can help you out! What about snow removal or lawn care? Longer driveways, and wider green spaces, will mean more work or more costs if you aren't doing these things on your own. Extra time to tend to these matters means less time for your work, family and the lifestyle that you may be looking for.

The allure of country living is undeniably strong, but the extra costs, time and knowledge you need to have are worth considering. Country living is more than just fresh air and green space!

Shivana Shamseer

Shivana's passion for real estate started long before she obtained her real estate license. Shivana spent over a decade buying and redeveloping many residential properties in the Greater Toronto Area with family, friends, and fellow investors. Some projects were small-scale cosmetic clean-ups, while others were full-scale overhauls of a property, all while retaining her full-time job at a large Canadian bank. These projects truly were a passion of hers to redevelop and redesign, finding fascination in remarkable transformations that occurred from start to finish of each property.

As friends, families, and neighbours walked through her re-development projects, they often inquired if she could work with them to design new features like kitchens and bathrooms in their homes. In 2016 she formed "Red Door Designs by Shivana" just to take on those projects and work, which eventually led to her leaving her job at the bank to take on design and construction projects full-time.

Always searching for ways to learn more and grow her business, Shivana earned her Real Estate license in 2020 to branch out and expand her desire to work with more families.

Prior to jumping into the real estate game, Shivana worked at a large Canadian bank for over ten years in various analytical roles. Shivana has spent many years developing her investment analysis skills. Shivana uses her investment and analytical skills, along with real estate market knowledge, to help guide her clients and assess each home to ensure they are getting the property that best meets their needs and expected returns. This comes especially handy when working with her real estate investors to grow their portfolios and advise them on the best-performing assets in their portfolio and how to best re-position themselves to generate their expected returns to build wealth for the future.

This added value of an agent who has been an entrepreneur for so many years, always finding ways to add value to her projects and properties, brings a lot of confidence and strong analytical skills to the table for any discerning client. She also comes with a very personal approach to each client and their plan to get from where they are to where they want to be in the time that they want.

In her spare time, Shivana loves to get outdoors with her son, for walks and bike rides in the neighbourhood, forest trail hikes, or finding time to be near and in the water; they love to enjoy time together. Together they love cooking new things in the kitchen, trying new restaurants, and following favourite chefs online to see what they are cooking up next!

You can follow her on Social Media here:

Instagram: https://bit.ly/3teHmss

Facebook: https://bit.ly/3EdMqDE

Tiktok: http://bit.ly/3A0nEEi

YouTube: http://bit.ly/3Yco97q

Or on her website at: www.soldwithshivana.com or by email at sales@ssrealtypartners.com

MARITAL SETTLEMENT AGREEMENT

Rose Rezaei

One of the most productive methods for couples to move forward with a divorce and on with their lives is to disconnect emotionally and handle the sale of the home in a business manner. Because the marital home is usually the greatest asset in a marriage, it is also the greatest liability.

You must give a lot of serious thought to securing settlement terms that protect both parties, especially the spouse who is departing the home. When you enter into your marital settlement agreement, your lawyer should specify who is Financially responsible for the mortgage, the homeowner's insurance, utilities, and upkeep of the marital home.

If the spouse occupying the marital home is responsible for listing, showing, and selling the home, the other spouse may be obligated to pay part or all f the mortgage, as well as contribute to the upkeep of the home. If the occupying spouse shows little effort in getting the house sold, the marital agreement should provide a timetable for the sale of the home.

It is important for the marital agreement to include provisions outlining the stops to be taken if the house cannot be sold within a specified time or if one spouse fails to meet any financial obligations.

Consult your legal adviser for contingencies that are specific to your situation. Additional expenses may include repainting, landscaping, or replacing appliances or carpeting.

There should be clear direction on how to handle the unexpected while in the process of selling the home - for example, if a home inspection reveals a cracked foundation or termite infestation. Ex-spouses sometimes agree to a fixed amount of time to share expenses prior to the sale of the home.

Quick decisions can be damaging especially when it comes to co-ownership or one spouse occupying the home until it sells. By keeping emotions at bay while making important decisions and focusing on what needs to be done to sell your home, you and your ex-spouse can move on faster.

HAVE REASONABLE AND REALISTIC EXPECTATIONS

Since the home is one of the most valuable marital assets, dividing the property between a couple in the throes of divorce can be a major source of contention.

If you have other properties, such as a vacation home or investment properties, those will also have to be assessed and assigned a monetary value. In order to divide equitably or equally, as the case may be, you will need to know the precise value of your property.

When it comes to the marital home, there are several common valuation methods available to determine the value. These are used in property settlements and may differ from what you perceive as your home's worth.

The other processes you should do are:

Comparative Market Analysis

Broker Price Opinion

The Cost Approach

Professional Appraisal

Finding The Right Realtor

Rose Rezaei

Rose Rezaei is a successful real estate agent who has been in the industry for several years. With her expertise, she has helped numerous clients buy, sell, and rent both commercial and residential properties. Her knowledge of the market, negotiation skills, and attention to detail have earned her a reputation as a top-performing agent.

Prior to her career in real estate, Rose was a principal of a high school in her hometown. She is also a successful businesswoman, having owned and operated a beauty clinic. Her experience in managing the Rosetty team and running a successful business has been invaluable in her real estate career.

Currently, Rose is focused on helping her husband with their new catering business called Finger Food Factory. As a team, they are working hard to provide quality food and excellent service to their clients.

Rose is a driven individual who is passionate about helping others achieve their goals. Her diverse background and experiences have made her a well-rounded professional and an asset to the real estate industry.

To contact Rose :

f 🐦 📹 in 🄾 🅿 rosetty.ca

email: Info@rosetty.ca

Mobile: (416) 520-2382

Mobile: (647) 606-2076

—

Clueless – My Journey of Becoming the 4th Generation to Venture into Real Estate

Yvette C. Owens

Several pivotal moments in my life have been unforeseen and powerfully changed my trajectory. In every instance, I am always surprised and somewhat baffled by how these moments sneak up on me when I am always planning and driving to achieve. Perhaps this is why God loves redirecting me, especially once I know my direction. After reaching my age, one would think that I would learn to rest in pursuing my vision and goal while still leaving room for the unexpected by the one and only God. Each time I encounter a new and unexpected path, I remember the following:

1) He has a definite plan for my entire life.

2) He is very much invested and involved in the outcome.

"What's meant to be will always find a way." – Trisha Yearwood. (American singer, actress, author, TV personality, and married to Garth Brooks)

I had a vivid dream about my maternal great-grandmother. I grew up around her as a child. Grandma Jones was a true matriarch. She birthed one child, a daughter. However, my great-grandmother, Annie M. Jones, fostered over 90 children. I was 12 years old when she transitioned to glory.

I remember representatives from Baltimore acknowledged her loving care for all those children. I grew up knowing many of those she cared for as Aunts and Uncles. Our family is naturally large in that my grandmother had nine children. My great-grandmother was a believer in Christ and taught us to serve Him all the days of our lives actively. She was a very proud and dominant woman. My great-grandfather, who died before I was born, was a strong, quiet man known for his beautiful landscaping.

What I learned about my great-grandmother is that she owned multiple properties which she rented. My Aunt told me about my great-grandmother's real estate investments when I went on a quest to understand my dream.

You can imagine the relief I experienced when I learned about her real estate ventures. I thought the dream was preparing me to become a foster parent because that is what I knew about my great-grandmother.

Honestly, I was not looking forward to fostering children. God bless those who nurture children and who do it well. It just wasn't for me. I know the challenging emotional, physical, and financial work involved. In today's environment, fostering can be even more complex at times. I breathed a sigh of relief to learn of another dimension of my great-grandmother. So what does this mean for me?

I am a 63-year-old single black woman preparing for retirement. As many do at this stage, I began researching other income streams to allow me to live the lifestyle I desire. After a divorce, raising my daughter, helping my siblings, and in recent years my 86-year-old Mom, I need options beyond the savings and retirement funds from my past and current employers.

Airbnbs are appealing to me. I asked my circle's most successful real estate expert about the best practices for setting up an Airbnb. I want to keep my living space private. However, the cute little homes in my area would make great AirBNBs.

During our conversation, I shared my dream about my great-grandmother and how it led me to learn about her real estate portfolio. My friend, in shock, said, "Yvette, I had the same dream about my grandmother." My friend had never shared her dream with anyone.

The life-altering question was, "Yvette do you want to join my team?" You see, my friend relocated to another state and didn't believe she should walk away from the lucrative business she built as a result of much hard work. We both felt so much in this divine moment that it made my decision easier.

You may ask, "Why did you have to take time to decide if this was the right opportunity for you?" Here's why. I work a full-time job; I launched a leadership and organization development company several years ago; I am active in my church as a minister and worship leader. My family is significant to me; I help my siblings care for my Mom long distance, and I have the privilege of helping my daughter and my two grandchildren.

I strive for excellence in everything, and taking on another significant business seemed overwhelming, especially as I am still laying the foundation to leave a rich, healthy legacy. I must do all I can to ensure an incredible ROI and ROE.

In an *Indeed* article, Dave Lee explains the difference between Return on Equity (ROE) vs. Return on Investment (ROI) in a way I can understand.

"Each ratio serves a different purpose when informing financial experts about a company's monetary status. Return on equity measures how effectively a company manages the money its investors and shareholders contribute. Its focus is strategic financial management within a company. ROI measures the profitability of an investment for the company. It can help predict the potential

monetary return a company may receive if it invests money in a particular business venture." ~ Dave Lee

The questions swirling in my head were, "Can I do it all successfully and not give up on what I already built in my business?" "Where is the extra capacity coming from?" "Will I receive pressure to produce beyond my ability considering all that is on my plate?" "Why is this now coming up? It was not on my radar or vision board, not specifically.

Have you asked yourself these or similar questions when taking on something new? I was nervous and still said, "Yes." I only had some of the answers to my questions when deciding. I knew this was pivotal for me and my family's future. I had to move forward despite not knowing how this would work out. I had to trust that this plan for me was another one God would watch over to perform until the day of Jesus Christ's return.

I contemplate the legacy I am building for my family and me and the families I help find the best property. There will not be another generation or more in my family who will need to be more knowledgeable about our legacy in real estate.

It's funny how a few cousins, aunts, and uncles flipped homes and owned multiple properties, and we never tied it to a multigenerational calling to the real estate industry. Hindsight is straightforward and gives me chill bumps thinking about the divine trail through our heritage. I will continue to share our story and encourage the next generation in this vein.

Here is why I will insist the legacy lives on. Everyone must be respected and deserve the right to a professional to help locate their next home. It can be frustrating when the client is demanding, yet their finances will not support them. My biggest lesson learned is to be more rational with my clients' choices or funds. I am efficient in weighing my options. However, I found that some people choose to live on a friend's couch until they get a place that fits their requirements. I want a clean space and to stop living out of boxes.

I had a client with the image of her last apartment in her mind. She imagined an area large enough to fit her past furniture, which she no longer possessed. Convincing her that she could be comfortable in a smaller place was received poorly. My job as a real estate agent was to help buyers consider all the options. I now know that I am here to give the clients the best options and as much information as possible so they can make an informed decision.

The best part of being a real estate agent is making the journey to owning and selling property full of grace and ease. People are vulnerable when selling and purchasing property. Other life situations are happening simultaneously, like the woman looking for a home for her brother, who lives out of state. He was returning to be closer to her after the recent death of their last parent. This sweet woman wept as she shared how her brother desired to be here for her as they aged together.

On a cold Saturday morning, she viewed a second-floor condo limping due to a bad hip that awaited surgery. The middle-aged woman was also restricted by what she could purchase and hung on to my every word because this was her first property purchase. She felt she only had one shot at this due to her age — the gentleman had to remind his wife of the potential of properties.

Their unique future use of the choice property required them to select a renovation property. Each family has a story that pulls my heart into the transaction and causes me to provide comfort and encouragement, which gives me great joy.

I am a 42-career corporate warrior. My mantra is that we must put our hearts back into the business. The culture does not have to be dog-eat-dog. The level of energy that it takes to be treacherous, evil-spirited, and overly competitive is exhausting to me. I want my clients to love the process of purchasing a home, love their new home, and love me for serving them so well. My best foot forward is the norm for every interaction with me. When my buyers and sellers get the best deal, I can negotiate for them; I am ecstatic.

Real estate pushed me out of my comfort zone into a phase of more learning. I can only expect to enter this role if I know what to do or learn everything quickly. Sitting for the state and national exams convinced me it would take time to learn and master real estate's mindset, practices, and technical sides. I have to be patient with myself during the learning process. Trying to look professional is tough when you are unsure of many things. Clients are looking to me for the answers they must rely on others to give. The potential clients who test my knowledge have a right to do so to ensure I represent them well.

The most incredible legacy we can build is one full of options built upon our achievements and explicit expectations to expand our lineage far beyond what we could imagine. I am committed to helping you become vetted with new ownership or assisting you in selling your current property.

I am a world-renowned speaker, international best-selling author, and leadership coach/consultant who teaches leaders the principles of change leadership to increase adoption, retain talent, and build high-performing teams using the proprietary V.I.C.T.O.R. framework.

When I am not wearing the above hats, I am a Mom to my beautiful daughter and my five gifted adult godchildren. I am the grandmother of my amazing grandson and granddaughter.

Here are some things you can expect as we work together:

Organized project management

Timely communication

Proactive regarding your interests

Celebrating your success

I look forward to assisting you achieve your real estate goals.

REAL ESTATE INSIDE OUT

Yvette C. Owens

Yvette C. Owens is a world-renowned speaker, international best-selling author, and leadership coach/consultant who teaches leaders the principles of change leadership to increase adoption, retain talent, and build high-performing teams using the V.I.C.T.O.R. framework.

She is the "Business Ambassador" for DestinySpeakInc. helping leaders create Healthy Cultures through Strategic Change.

Yvette is a board-certified professional (A.C.M.P.) with 40+ years of sharing her vibrance, resilience, compassion, and influence in teaching "Dealing with Resistance to Accept and Invest in Change" during keynote speeches and live and virtual working sessions.

1-800-778-8524

destinyspeakv2r@gmail.com

destinyspeak.com

Facebook: @DestinySpeakV2R

Twitter: @YvetteOwens1

BIZSHUI - FOR REAL ESTATE

Claire Boscq

What if Feng Shui could help you sell your real estate quicker?

Did you know that it takes seven seconds for someone to make a first impression of you or of a place? Well, yes... hence why it is crucial to make that first impression count.

How a property looks will affect the way a prospective buyer feels about a home; that split second when they walk in, and somehow it does not feel right, they will not buy it, or it does, and you don't even have to show them around, they know in their guts, it is the right house for them.

Environmental psychology, the scientific study of the interrelationships between people and their physical surroundings, shows why our environment impacts us, how we can leverage that knowledge to our advantage, and what we can do to improve our relationship with the world around us? Furthermore, research from Somatic psychotherapy demonstrates how our mind-body connection has a direct correlation to our states, our feelings, thoughts and behaviour.

So, our environment affects our state and our state affects our behaviour. Simple right? Healthy, harmonious environments, mean happy, relaxed, creative, feel-good people, which means a more fulfilled lifestyle.

Creating harmony and flow is what Feng Shui does. The purpose of Feng Shui is to make people feel good by promoting an effective use, not only of your space and materials but an alignment of the flow of energy with your own state. With some simple home adjustments, you can improve the overall presentation and feel of your home and maximize its value.

Feng Shui originated in China; it is a traditional Eastern philosophy, a belief system in which there is a spiritual relationship between the physical elements of nature and human-made environments to create the right balance of energy for harmony in one's space. It might not be the first thing that comes to your mind for improving your home when selling it, but it's an indirect way to improve feelings and behaviours from the buyers' perspective.

Did you know that 95% of our decisions are made subconsciously? - Gerald Zaltman

According to cognitive neuroscientists, we are conscious of only about 5 percent of our cognitive activity, so most of our decisions, actions, emotions, and behaviour depends on the 95 percent of brain activity that goes beyond our conscious awareness. Humans are driven by feeling, so emotions are what really drive the purchasing behaviours and also, decision-making in general. So, if you want your buyers to buy a property, you must connect with them on an emotional level.

But how does it work then, all of those emotions? I am not a neuroscientist, but here is a quick Neuroscience round-up.

In a very simple way, we have two sides of our brain. The left side of the brain, the neocortex brain or masculine energy or yang energy, helps us tell 'what we do.' It is responsible for performing tasks that have to do with logic; it is also responsible for rational and analytical thoughts and language; it is the sales figures, the action, and the 'let's go and do it' attitude.

On the other hand, the right hemisphere, the limbic brain or feminine energy/yin energy, helps us tell our story, our 'why we do what we do'; it performs tasks that have do with receptivity, such as that creative moment in the shower when you go EUREKA! It tells us about our emotions, motivation and feelings, such as trust and loyalty.

In recap, the neocortex allows us to look through vast amounts of facts and figures, but it doesn't drive behaviour. The limbic brain drives most behaviour, and this is where we experience emotions; then, it makes sense since people would make decisions based on emotions. They will then back up those decisions with the neocortex part of their brain.

To sell anything, a home or a hoover, you need to connect directly with your buyers' emotion drivers and enhancing energy flow has a direct effect on the limbic brain and how people feel. Therefore, let me share with you how you can do that in 9 simple Feng Shui Moves:

Remove clutter

Clutter blocks the flow of energy (also called chi) throughout a home, and when chi can't flow naturally, it becomes stagnant. It's like damming up a river and preventing it from flowing down a mountainside. Keeping your space clear will keep the energy moving and keep opportunities coming in. Everything has energy in its frequency, so if you have items that have a negative representation or look out of place, it reduces the chance of the buyer imagining himself living there.

Make a WOW first impression

Start outside and look around the entrance. Is it inviting? Is it clearly signposted? Is it easily accessible? Can you see the front door? The door is the entrance of the chi; it is where good energy and luck enter our lives. So, keep doorways clear – front and back. Make sure all doorways aren't blocked and you can open the door in full. Clean Your Windows! The windows represent the 'eyes' of your home and affect your ability to see clearly, have clarity in the direction of your life and make decisions. Dirty windows can also mean that you can struggle to see and think clearly about your current life situation and what you are moving towards!

Use your Five Senses

Neuroscientists across the globe have studied images of the brain in action and placed emotions in the driver's seat, asserting that thinking is emotion-based, and while emotions form the basis of thoughts, the five senses of sight, sound, smell, taste and touch fuel those emotions, wielding power to persuade, relax and heal. When we walk into a room or space and instantly feel at ease and comfortable, we're likely enveloped by a balance of all five senses. Our nervous systems absorb that diaphanous energy — and we just feel better.

One of the most powerful senses, smell, is particularly important when selling a home. It can trigger associations and draw upon fond memories of other smells. Customers' olfactory sense will augment the Customer Experience; this is all part of the subconscious Experience. According to Rachel Herz, professor of psychiatry and human behaviour and author of the book *"The Scent of Desire"*, a smell is just a scent until a person associates it with a specific experience. After the association, the smell becomes a representation of that experience in the mind of the person. So be sure to diffuse essential oils or bake fresh bread before any visit.

Balance each room

Yin and yang are essentially the building blocks for all energy that we know of in the universe. Everything else comes out of these two types of energy.

Yin and yang describe the paradoxical unity of duality. You may have heard of the law of polarity. Masculine energy is doing, thinking, logical, and aggressive, while the feminine counterpart is being, creating, intuitive and passive.

Having a harmonious balance of both Yin and Yang Feng Shui forces in a home will create the quality of energy you need in order to live a happy life. This means some areas should have more yin or yang energies based on their purpose within a home.

Examples: a bedroom is a place of rest, love, and serenity; you will want to have more Yin energy in that area. Your kitchen, instead, is where the family gets nourished, laughs, and gets together; you want a lot more yang energy there.

Create abundant and supportive spaces

Feng Shui is based on the idea that all things in our environment, including inanimate objects, are instilled with some type of movement. The Five-Element theory, according to which the elements of wood, fire, earth, metal and water symbolize the five basic processes of nature and represent the five qualities of natural phenomena. The Chinese knew that by bringing nature inside, they would increase their feel-good mood, so creating a balanced and supportive space by incorporating nature and each of the five elements into the home will infuse the space with the positive energy and life of the outdoor world.

Repair, fix, get rid!

Throw away all objects that are broken, out of date, leaking faucets, broken glass, locks, latches, loose tiles, damaged equipment and appliances - really anything that has a negative association, as they contribute negative energy and block positive energy. Although you can try to replace and repair them, the best we can do is throw them out and ask yourself if they are broken or not working, "Do I really need to replace this item?" Got squeaky hinges? Oh no, it's a 'crying' door; with every swing open and shut, it dispenses a whiny vibe throughout your house, get your WD40 out and stop the whining!

Add plants

Plants represent the wood element, which encourages flexibility, growth, and compassion. Plants also add vibrant life energy to a space, so they are a great addition if you want to reinvigorate a certain area of your home or life. Plants suck up electromagnetic pollution, plus they transform and filter carbon monoxide into oxygen. The Peace Lily is an effective way of cleansing the air and neutralizing common pollutants such as formaldehyde. Formaldehyde is used in particle board or pressed wood products to make office or household furniture, in carpets, permanent pressed clothes, water repellents and fire retardants.

Reduce EMF

Electronic Magnetic Field (EMF) or technostress has been defined as the negative psychological link between people and the introduction of new technologies, affecting mental health. That high-energy radiation is not seen, but can be felt, the anxiety expressed by those experiencing technostress: insomnia, loss of temper, irritability, frustration and can increase errors in judgement and poor job performance if not dealt with. Our environment is full of a wide spectrum of electromagnetic radiation, from computers, mobile phones and masts, radio and TV broadcasts, WiFi, Bluetooth, power lines, domestic wiring, and other electrical appliances. When showing a property, turn off any plugs, TV, and power that are unused.

Stir up some chi

The fastest way to 'wake up' a home is to open all doors and windows, especially if it isn't lived in. Change the air before showing the home, move the energy by moving 27 things around; this is the quickest and simplest adjustment you could do.

You could pick up the 27 objects and put them right back where they were, clean or dust, move to the left or right, get rid of 27 items;

any of those will work - so take action, move some CHI in the house – both literally and symbolically!

The goal and key to Feng Shui are to create a balanced energy. Simply apply the above Feng Shui real estate tips, and the emotional value of the home will be considerably enhanced.

Make it more desirable, and you will increase the chances of selling a house fast and for a higher price!

Even if you don't have a plethora of buyers that follow the principles of Feng Shui, it's easy to see that a few of these tips and tricks would be useful for any seller trying to impress a group of buyers nonetheless. As any homeowner knows, you get a positive gut feeling of "yes, this could be the one!". These principles allow a seller to showcase their home in a minimalistic, clutter-free and harmonious manner that would have any skeptic turning to a Feng Shui convert (and possibly signing the dotted line on an offer on the home).

Claire Boscq

Claire Boscq is an Award-Winning Customer Experience Expert, Global Keynote Speaker, The BizShui™ Creator, inspiring organizations to enhance workplaces, increase customer experience and optimize employees' productivity.

She is the No. 1 woman on the Global customer experience gurus list with three decades of expertise; Claire is an authority in the customer experience industry.

International best-seller author with four published books, she is an international media influencer with her work published in Brazil, the Philippines, India, the US and Europe.

Claire has spoken in over 20 countries; she delivers fast-paced and high-energy presentations in French and English. Winner of the Institute of director award, she is also on the board of Virtual Speaker Association.

She brings a more holistic and comprehensive approach to organizations and individuals with her BizShui™ Method; creating powerful flow in businesses by integrating a blend of the traditional Feng Shui principles with modern business and personal needs turning people and places into prosperity. Now she isn't restricted to a zoom room; there is no stopping her from travelling around the world again!

https://www.linkedin.com/in/claireboscq/
https://www.youtube.com/c/ClaireBoscq
https://twitter.com/ClaireBoscq
https://www.facebook.com/claireboscqkeynotespeaker
https://www.instagram.com/claireboscq/
https://clubhousedb.com/user/claireboscq
https://www.claireboscq.com/

www.ingramcontent.com/pod-product-compliance
Lightning Source LLC
Chambersburg PA
CBHW071015120626
46546CB00003B/1099